MW01053968

# SUYAMA

## A COMPLEX SERENITY

Grant Hildebrand | Foreword by Glenn Murcutt

MARQUAND BOOKS, SEATTLE

IN ASSOCIATION WITH

UNIVERSITY OF WASHINGTON PRESS, SEATTLE AND LONDON

*Publication of* Suyama: A Complex Serenity *is made possible through the generous support of many long-time friends and clients of Suyama Peterson Deguchi and the University of Washington Press.*

University of Washington Press
P.O. Box 50096, Seattle, WA 98145 U.S.A.
www.washington.edu/uwpress

Library of Congress Cataloging-in-Publication Data
Hildebrand, Grant, 1934–
  Suyama : a complex serenity / Grant Hildebrand ; foreword by Glenn Murcutt.
     p. cm.
  Includes index.
  ISBN 978-0-295-99081-1 (alk. paper)
  1. Suyama, George Yosuke, 1942-—Themes, motives. 2. Suyama Peterson Deguchi (Firm) 3. Architecture—United States—History—20th century.
4. Architecture—United States—History—21st century.  I. Suyama, George Yosuke, 1942– II. Title.
NA737.S923A4 2011
720.92—dc22                                    2010050011

The paper used in this publication meets the minimum requirements of American National Standard for Information Sciences—Permanence of Paper for Printed Library Materials, ANSI Z39.48-1984.∞

Produced by Marquand Books, Inc., Seattle
   www.marquand.com

Edited by Marilyn Trueblood
Designed by Jeff Wincapaw
Typeset in DIN by Tina Henderson
Proofread by Carrie Wicks
Color Management by iocolor, Seattle
Printed and bound in China by Artron Color Printing Co., Ltd.

# Contents

# Foreword

In the early years of the twenty-first century the architectural profession seems obsessed with computer-generated and manipulated forms. Many designs fail to observe structural logic, for no better reason than that they can do so—sloping, twisting, leaning, flaunting an illusion of defiance of gravity; some make the disaster of a rail smash seem ordered. Such an architecture, claiming to stimulate the visual senses, becomes tiresome in its pointless striving, while it squanders the earth's precious resources.

It is a welcome relief to find architects who continue to search for an architecture that is appropriate and relevant to time, place, and culture, an architecture of response rather than imposition. Such is the work of the firm founded in 1971 as George Suyama, Architect, which, with the addition of partners Ric Peterson in 1983 and Jay Deguchi in 2003, now practices as Suyama Peterson Deguchi.

In the years from 1945 to 1966, *Arts and Architecture*, an American magazine based in Los Angeles, sponsored the design of thirty-six houses, largely in the Los Angeles region, by architects who had attained, or would attain, distinguished reputations. These designs were known as the Case Study Houses. Their influence went well beyond the United States, and well beyond their own time. For many architects, the ideas realized in those designs have remained relevant for more than sixty years, during which time a number of other movements in architecture have come and gone.

Suyama Peterson Deguchi's work combines the spirit and authentic quality of the Case Study Houses, with influences from Japan and from the history, culture, craft, and materials of the Pacific Northwest. Their innovative work is an enduring contemporary architecture of beautiful proportions and human scale, superbly constructed from a palette of materials integrated by detailing of remarkable finesse. Each building works closely with its site, taking into account the vagaries of the local climate; the wind patterns over landforms and waterways; the latitude, altitude, and proximity to water; the geomorphology, geology, topography, and ground and surface water patterns; the flora; and the orientation, aspect and prospect.

The buildings generally do not give any indication of what lies beyond the entry frontage, the occupant's privacy always being retained. A sequence of spaces develops from the public realm to the semi-public to the private. In this temperate, moist, coastal climate of the Northwest, roofed, open-sided courtyard spaces develop into verandahs providing small glimpses of distant views. Not until one enters the main interior space is the broader landscape revealed. Walkways and verandahs are given generous eaves that provide security and protection against the seasonal inclement weather without compromising the soft light of the region. Interiors offer places of refuge during the long winter months, while with the long daylight hours of summer, the roofed outside spaces become daytime and evening external living areas, many of them overlooking the most beautiful waterways of the region.

Working closely with landscape architects, Suyama Peterson Deguchi ensure that their serene interiors work seamlessly with nature and the land, blurring boundaries between the interiors and the courtyards, verandahs, and gardens. Walls, decks, paving, ground textures, rocks, water, grasslands, and variously colored, textured, and scaled flora reinforce the connection between building and landscape. Water is also used, both statically and actively, as a connecting element, weaving its way alongside entry spaces and adjacent to primary and secondary rooms, through sequences of still ponds, running and falling water. The water emits varying sounds, and washes walls and ceilings with shimmering reflections from the undulating surface.

Such work reveals a dedication, a commitment to excellence, in architect, client, and builder. This superb architecture, seemingly regional, has a universal significance.

**Glenn Murcutt, Architect**
Order of Australia
Alvar Aalto Medal, RAIA Gold Medal, AIA Gold Medal, Pritzker Prize

# Acknowledgments

Pat Soden, director of the University of Washington Press, and Lee Soper, a key figure in the history of the University Book Store, proposed the idea of this book and asked me if I would be interested in authoring it. No request could have been more welcome. I thank them for their invitation and for their unwavering support throughout the book's development. I am grateful to Pat for his selection of Ed Marquand for the book's design; no one is more distinguished in his field. I thank Ed as well for assigning the project's development to Jeff Wincapaw, whose talent and attention have yielded a design commensurate in elegance with that of its subject.

One can write about a building without actually experiencing it, and when it no longer exists or has been radically changed, there is no alternative. But architecture entails the composing of spaces and sequences of spaces; it involves the management of light in both its quantitative and qualitative aspects; it is often accompanied by audial and olfactory sensations. Thus in writing about a building, the experience of it in its actuality is of enormous value. It follows that I am much indebted to Lyn and Gerald Grinstein, Frances and Scott McAdams, Laurie and George Schuchart, Kim and George Suyama, Janet and Gene Zema, and the owners of the Orchard, all of whom graciously allowed me to experience their homes, without restrictions or preconditions.

Bruce Hinckley, Ric Peterson, and Jay Deguchi have openly discussed all aspects of their most important role in the story. The office staff have been equally helpful; in that regard I must mention especially Jym Snedeker, Sarah MacDonald, Debi Yeabsley, Steven Lazen, who spent long hours obtaining and organizing the images for the book, and Emma Shultz, who also spent long hours compiling the lists of significant projects and contributing personnel. Kim Suyama read the manuscript on several occasions and made significant additions and corrections. Larry Rouch talked with me at length about the project and contributed major ideas on both the organization and the content of the book. Marilyn Trueblood, managing editor of the Press, suggested a number of most helpful organizational improvements. Nina McGuinness found the invaluable donors who made the production possible. Finally, I want to acknowledge two most valued contributors to this project: Glenn Murcutt, who with his usual kind enthusiasm provided a foreword to the text, and Miriam, without whom I much suspect I could not have written this book. I am most grateful to all of the above. Their contributions have much to do with the strengths of this book; its weaknesses must be assigned to me.

G. H.

# Introduction

In 1792 George Vancouver, exploring the deep, salt waters that open southward from the Strait of Juan de Fuca, named the sound for Peter Puget, one of his officers, and gave the surrounding region, bounded on the west by the Olympic Mountains and on the east by the Cascades, over four hundred of its still-used place names. Puget Sound's labyrinthine bays, channels, and inlets harbor a plethora of fish and shellfish, while the moderate climate and the generous rainfall nurture, on the lands around, a remarkable diversity of plants, which in turn nurture a wide variety of animal species. Until recent times, the same moderate and wet climate supported the densest forest stands on the continent, from which the indigenous peoples built their durable shelters—the Northwest Coast tribes' canonical two- and six-beam houses and their communal longhouses.

Immigrant settlers first appeared on the shores of Puget Sound in 1851, landing on the tip of a peninsula projecting into what Vancouver had named Elliott Bay. They called their settlement New York Alki; *alki* was a Chinook word meaning, roughly, by-and-by. The settlers soon moved eastward to the mouth of the Duwamish River and renamed their settlement Seattle, after the local Suquamish chief who befriended them.[1] As the indigenous peoples had done, so too these early immigrant settlers built their buildings of wood, and made it the staple of their economy.

In the 1860s Chinese came from California to settle in the area south of Seattle's downtown known as Chinatown, now known as the International District. Discovery of gold in the Yukon in 1897 brought adventurers from all corners of the earth, and many of them, stopping in the region to earn funds for the rest of the journey, went no farther. These immigrants included a large number of Scandinavians, who settled among the drying stacks of fir and cedar from the Ballard neighborhood's mills. Then, in the early decades of the twentieth century, the Japanese began to arrive. George Suyama's grandparents were among them, settling first in Tacoma, then moving, after several years, to Seattle. The Japanese came in such numbers that by 1930, when Seattle's "Chinatown" included some 12,000 inhabitants, the majority were persons of Japanese descent and Japanese businesses dominated the district's commerce. With the advent of World War II, these people, like all others of Japanese ancestry in the western states, were sent to internment camps and their businesses were seized or abandoned, in many cases never to be reestablished.

In the decades that followed the close of that war, there appeared around the sound a distinctive body of architecture entirely manifested in small buildings—suburban medical clinics, neighborhood libraries, modest houses—often sensitively related to dramatic sites. The buildings were modernist in that they were entirely free of any features drawn from past architectural examples. Their most evident characteristic was a profuse use of wood, both as exposed structure and as an interior and exterior surfacing material, always left either in its natural state or with a slight protective stain. Roofs were pitched, more often than not, with significant overhangs, in response to the prevalent rain. Windows were generous for the same reason, and to claim the striking views available from often remarkable sites. The movement was influenced by the early-twentieth-century architecture of Charles and Henry Greene, Bernard Maybeck, and Ernest Coxhead in California, by the more modest work of Ellsworth Storey in Seattle from 1903 onward, and by the late-1930s work of Pietro Belluschi and John Yeon in Oregon. And, oddly, considering the bitterness engendered by the war, the style was deeply influenced by images of Japan's vernacular architecture brought home by many returning GIs and by the Puget Sound region's long history of a Japanese presence. The best-known architect of the movement was Paul Hayden Kirk; others included Ralph Anderson, Albert Bumgardner, Arne Bystrom, Alan Liddle, Royal McClure, Omer Mithun, Robert Billsborough Price, and Gene Zema.

George Suyama was born in Seattle in 1942, spent the first three years of his life interned in an Idaho camp, completed grade school and high school in Seattle, graduated from the architecture program at the University of Washington in 1967, and found his first architectural employment with Gene Zema. Zema's work, though less well known than that of many of his colleagues, is unexampled in its spatial and formal complexity, its flawless interrelationship of structure, materials, space, and form, and its luxuriant detailing. Suyama believes that that first job and his later friendship with Zema were the foundations of his development as an architect. For many years Suyama's designs, strongly influenced by Zema's, were themselves outstanding representatives of the Northwest Style.

With the passing of the decades, the region changed. Tacoma, the butt of jokes in the immediate post-war years, transformed itself into a thriving, exciting metropolis. Bellevue, before the war hardly a crossroads, became the state's fourth-largest city. Seattle is still not New York *alki*, but Microsoft, Starbucks, Nordstroms, Washington Mutual, and Amazon have become national and international household words. Boeing, builder of the famous bombers of World War II, has been since the 1960s the world's dominant builder of large passenger aircraft; Air Force One is and has long been a Boeing product. The University of Washington, once a provincial institution, is now one of the nation's premier universities and has been for decades the recipient of more federal research moneys than any other school in the country, public or private.[2] The great forests, however, are largely gone, and wood for architectural construction is now typically "engineered wood" and "particle board," composites of the wood chips and sawdust that once were sawmill waste. The hallmarks of the Northwest Style—exposed structural members of fine woods, walls and ceilings of cedar and vertical grain fir—are now rarely possible, and only with extraordinary budgets.

George Suyama continues to use wood, but in more limited areas and not in all projects, and much of what he does use is engineered wood and particle board. He has increasingly turned to an architecture of metals and concrete. His details have evolved from the exuberant to the meticulously distilled. Yet his forms and spaces still find their sources in the intrinsic determinants of architecture: the nature of the material (whatever it may be), the site, the climate, the needs and wishes of the client, and the character of the region. Suyama is quick to acknowledge that his work draws, too, from the abilities of his associates, both within and outside his firm, and from the artist-craftsmen whose skills have enabled the execution of his designs. Although Suyama has spent his life in the Pacific Northwest, his work increasingly reveals deep associations with the recent and the more remote past of his ancestral Japan.

Suyama says he wishes to simplify, to eliminate visual noise. This is patent in his work: it exhibits no baroque gestures, no evident ostentation; trim, in any conventional sense, is nonexistent; the palette of materials is limited. Geometries are those of right angles and rectangular prisms, with here and there a sloping surface or an arc, but not many of them; Euclid would be at home with it all. All is simple.

Yet it isn't. On deeper examination, Suyama's architecture reveals a profusion of complexities, ambiguities, and multivalences—characteristics dear to postmodernists and deconstructionists. But his complexities, ambiguities, and multivalences yield neither postmodernist historicism nor deconstructionist conflict. Rather his architecture is one of intense, even exciting tranquility, because all is held within a pervasive order—the order he chooses to call simplicity. So it is that his quest to eliminate visual noise creates not visual silence but a kind of visual peace, a visual music. The analogy to music can be carried further: Suyama's means entail the distillation of architectural elements to a purity analogous to that of a musical tone, and relationships between those elements as pure and artistically rich as the mathematics of musical relationships. In these accomplishments he stands alone.

1. Known as Chief Sealth, he delivered in his namesake city, in January of 1854, a famous speech whose exact words still remain unknown. See Albert Furtwangler, *Answering Chief Seattle* (Seattle: University of Washington Press, 1997).
2. This includes MIT. The beginnings of the university's transformation are usually dated to the 1960s and to the presidency of Charles E. Odegaard, who took office in August 1958.

# 1 Origins

Shosaku Suyama came to Tacoma, Washington, from his native Takahashi in 1907, as a young man of eighteen. Over the next six years he eked out a livelihood at various jobs in various western Washington towns. In 1913, having married, perhaps by distant arrangement, he brought his wife, Sakuko, from Okayama, Japan, to Tacoma. Shortly after her arrival, they moved to Seattle, where Shosaku began selling produce at an open-air market on Western Avenue near the waterfront.[1] When their son, Shoichi, came of age, he joined his father in the business. In the late 1930s, Shoichi married Tomiko Saiki, and the four Suyamas and Tomiko's parents lived together as an extended family in the area, south of Yesler Way, known as the International District.

Shoichi and Tomiko's first child, George Yosuke Suyama, was born on February 22, 1942, two and a half months after the Japanese attack on Pearl Harbor and three days after President Roosevelt signed the executive order for internment of Japanese Americans in the Pacific Coast states and the seizure and sale of their property. By August the entire Suyama household had been interned at Minidoka, a camp thirteen miles due east of Jerome, Idaho, where temperatures ranged from 21 degrees below zero to 104 degrees above.[2] Newly built for its purpose, Minidoka housed more than nine thousand internees in thirty-six uninsulated, tarpaper barracks within a treeless, barren, and barbed-wire-fenced compound.[3] Tomiko's parents died in the camp; the Suyamas survived. When the camp was closed in September 1945, the family returned to Seattle. The camp years were never thereafter overtly mentioned in the home, but George recalls that the shame of the experience was an undercurrent in their lives; he believes, too, that it was the source of a prevailing precept, in the family and the community, that one must expect nothing, because all can be suddenly taken away. The experience also reinforced ethnic identity: "We were Japanese—and I am, still and always, Japanese."

On the Suyamas' return to Seattle, Shoichi was able to resume his produce business, but his father was now too frail to help; to supplement the income, Tomiko did catering and housekeeping for a clientele that included the Seattle Golf Club. With Shoichi and Tomiko both working, it was left to the elder Suyamas to tend the house and care for the children; George recalls that "grandfather was the patriarch, but grandmother was the one who really ran the family." He remembers Shosaku and Sakuko as "solid and calm," and recalls an axiom they often repeated: "one's actions reflect one's beliefs." George has especially strong, warm memories of his grandfather: he was "a very principled man, open and generous—he taught us that 'what you give to others will come back to you'—he would never fail to help others if help was needed or useful." So it happened that in the shaping of George's childhood, a generation was skipped: his imparted attitudes and beliefs resemble those of a second-generation Japanese American more than those of someone of his own third generation. Although his parents were a lesser presence in his early life, he remembers them as eminently pragmatic; accomplishments were more important to them than intellectual reflection.

In Seattle, George was sent to Bailey Gatzert Elementary School, then to Beacon Hill for grade school. He did not excel in his classwork, and he began to use art as a means of gaining recognition; he remembers doing a large and time-consuming mural for a special occasion, and he has kept some pottery pieces that he can still view without embarrassment.

Four siblings arrived in those post-camp years: Eileen in September of 1945, just days after the family's return to Seattle; Barbara in 1952, Deborah in 1955, and Scott in 1956.

From 1956 to 1960, George attended Franklin High School. "It was assumed that I would work every nonschool hour during the school year and full time every summer, and I did—there was to be no free time, no sports, no reading for pleasure." But it was increasingly evident that any reading, for pleasure or not, was difficult for him; although he was never tested for dyslexia, he believes that that may have been the problem. With the inevitable self-consciousness of adolescence, George was sharply aware of being Japanese in a Euro-American culture. Few cities in America, however, are less Eurocentric than Seattle, and George's ethnicity was apparently less important to his classmates than the appeal of his gregarious but self-effacing personality, because he was elected class president in his senior year. Although he uses no superlatives in describing his classroom accomplishments, Franklin was one of the more academically rigorous of Seattle's schools and George's record was sufficient to gain him admission to the University of Washington.

He began his studies there in the fall of 1960, in the College of Arts and Sciences.

George found himself a president again, this time of the university's freshman class, among whom he had a large number of friends. But unlike many who become architects, he had no clear sense of purpose at that time and no particular inclination for architecture. His mother had it in mind that he should be a doctor, and although his own heart wasn't in it, he doggedly pursued a pre-medical curriculum for two years. In his third year, he considered psychology; his clearest memories of that year are of long evenings—very long evenings—of existentialist conversations with a fellow student. George had left the family home at the beginning of his freshman year to rent his own apartment, and he had "decorated" it: he had painted the walls, doing a mural of the Seattle cityscape on one of them, and chosen and arranged furniture; he remembers a cherished oak icebox with brass handles that he bought at St. Vincent de Paul for fifty cents. He was working, too, at a men's store, Vaughan's, on University Way, whose proprietor "had a great eye for antiques," from which he created what George thought were remarkably beautiful rooms. He began to sense in himself an interest in design, and his roommate, Grant Allen, an architecture student, reinforced that interest. In the fall of 1963, in what would ordinarily have been the beginning of his senior year, George transferred from Arts and Sciences to the Department of Architecture in the College of Architecture and Urban Planning.

He entered at a time when the field was consciously and radically changing. Ten years earlier, the American architectural scene had been dominated by European modernism, and especially the modernism of Mies van der Rohe, but its very ubiquity had led many architects to seek ways of moving beyond its increasingly evident limitations. By 1960 Le Corbusier's revolutionary sculpture of mass, space, and light at Ronchamp and Paul Rudolph's theatrical School of Architecture at Yale had been completed. In the following year, Louis I. Kahn's Richards Medical Laboratories at the University of Pennsylvania appeared in publication after publication; articulated to distinguish "master" and "servant" spaces, the brick and concrete forms of Kahn's towers seemed as much ancient as modern. In the same year, in Orinda, California,

Charles Moore designed for himself a less publicized small house, whose neo-vernacular exterior of shingles and sliding barn doors enclosed an interior featuring two canopies on neo-Tuscan wood columns. Moore intended this project to challenge what he, and others, had begun to regard as the restrictive dogmas of modernism. Jane Jacobs's *Death and Life of Great American Cities* (1961) was to become the classic articulation of a growing concern for modernism's damage to the urban fabric,[4] and that concern was dramatically intensified by the demolition in 1964 of New York's Pennsylvania Station, McKim, Mead, and White's masterpiece and one of America's greatest buildings. Two years later, in *Complexity and Contradiction in Architecture*, Robert Venturi eloquently attacked a wide range of modernist tenets,[5] advocating a freedom of approach that could include historic references, willfulness, irony, even whimsy.

The tensions these events engendered in schools of architecture were exacerbated by other circumstances of the time, especially the increasingly resented Vietnam War. They were further exacerbated at the University of Washington by its particular circumstances. In the 1930s, 1940s, and to a much lesser degree the 1950s, the program there had been led by Lionel Pries, one of the great teachers of architecture of his time.[6] Pries taught by means of an Ecole des Beaux-Arts methodology, but he was familiar with the art and architecture of Polynesia, the Far East, South Asia, and native America, and he spent most of his summers in Mexico, where he saw the work of Miguel Covarrubias, Juan O'Gorman, and Diego Rivera. From those many realms of design knowledge, he imbued in his students a remarkably catholic awareness of design sources and influences, including modernism. Although he was formidable in personality, even intimidating, in his passion for architecture he imparted a warmth as well, and many who were then his students remember the hospitality and the rich ambience of gatherings at his home near the campus. His extraordinary presence shaped generations of graduates, including, in the 1930s, Paul Hayden Kirk, Minoru Yamasaki, and Victor Steinbrueck, and in the immediate postwar years, Fred Bassetti, Astra Zarina, Wendell Lovett, Gene Zema, and Arne Bystrom.

When Pries left the faculty in 1958, the teaching methodology of the Bauhaus had been prevalent for several years in almost all American schools of architecture, but largely because of Pries's legendary presence, Washington was one of the last schools to convert. The sometimes-bitter disputes that had accompanied that transition were not yet entirely forgotten when George entered the program in 1963. Thus the ubiquitous contentiousness of the 1960s within schools of architecture was in evidence at Washington to an unusual degree.

In those circumstances, George, unlike his predecessors of the Pries era, remembers few inspiring moments and no heroic role-models. Although in his earlier dabbling in psychology, he had participated in those evenings of existential dialectics, he did not find himself drawn by the oral intellectual disputes that were then rife in architecture studios, and the literature, difficult for anyone, remained especially so for him. He was more engaged by the tangible material determinants of architectural form. The design studio he remembers most clearly was one with a physical product: students were to design, and build at full scale, a chair. George went through the curriculum with alacrity, finishing the usual five-year program in four years, and graduated in 1967 with the professional degree of Bachelor of Architecture.[7]

In the last six months of his schooling, however, George was employed by Seattle architect Gene Zema, and he views this as his single most important educational experience. Zema was a 1950 graduate of the University of Washington, and so had studied under Lionel Pries. The quality of Zema's work was evident early on. Although he gave no attention to self-promotion, within three years of his graduation, his residential designs were finding recognition. His material of choice was wood, for structure, for opaque surfaces inside and out, and for trim, and it was invariably exposed, its visible connections crafted with care and a rigorous logic. The structural elements, however, evolved in close concert with a dramatic formal and spatial composition, each, in a sense, shaping the other, so his work typically possesses a seamless integration of form, space, structure, and material.

Zema built with his own hands many of the buildings he designed. These included much of his office on Eastlake Avenue and Boston

1.1 Gene Zema's office, Seattle, 1961–62: the courtyard, 2009.

1.2 Zema's office: the interior, 2009.

1.3 House for Gene and Janet Zema, Seattle, 1962–64;
the exterior from the west, 2009. Gene Zema, architect.

Street, where George worked (figs. 1.1 and 1.2), much of Zema's Seattle residence in the Laurelhurst neighborhood (fig. 1.3), and the entirety of his later complex of buildings for himself and his wife on Whidbey Island (figs. 1.4–1.8). One could learn from Zema, then, everything there was to learn about the elegant making of buildings from wood, and George learned much of it in those brief six months. And he learned a lot from Zema in another realm as well. "Before I met Gene, the Japan I knew from my parents and grandparents was a Japan of work and morality, ancestry and cultural traditions. Gene gave me my first glimpse of a Japanese aesthetic dimension." In fact, Zema gave George far more than a glimpse. The spatial complexities and the rich intimate detail of Zema's architecture must be assigned to his own inventiveness, but in his demand that the structure itself be the finely crafted visible ordering force of the building, his work is related not only to that of his compatriot contemporaries but to the best of traditional Japanese architecture as well. Furthermore, Zema had developed, early on, a deep familiarity with Japanese crafts, which had led him to acquire, by the mid-1960s, a significant collection of Japanese artifacts that included fabric arts,

farmhouse accoutrements, screens, temple and shrine ornamental details, swords, and samurai armor, all of museum quality. These were displayed in Zema's office, in which George worked daily for those six impressionable months. They were even more magnificently displayed in the unforgettable ambience of Zema's home, to which George was often invited (figs. 1.3, 1.4, and see figs. 1.5–1.8). George's time with Zema, then, was an introduction to the physical artifacts of George's ancestral land and, to a remarkable degree, an immersion in a design process that bore some resemblance to the traditional design processes of Japan. Those experiences would indelibly influence George's career.

Upon his graduation in June of 1967, George was called into the army for six months of basic training, as part of the reservist program by which one could then satisfy the military obligation. On his return to Seattle in January 1968, he found Zema deeply involved in the design of a new building for the university's College of Architecture and Urban Planning, an atypical and, in the end, enervating project that had begun before George's departure.[8] George found work instead in the office of Ralph Anderson, in residential design the most prolific architect of the

**1.4** Zema house, Seattle: the living space looking east, 2009.

**1.5** Zema house, Whidbey Island 1983–90: passage to the entry court.

**1.6** Zema house, Whidbey Island: the living room. The ambience, and the artifacts, though in a different setting, that introduced to Suyama the aesthetic of his ancestral land.

**1.7** Zema house, Whidbey Island: the master bedroom.

**1.8** Zema house, Whidbey Island: the Japanese tub room, with water wheel from Takayama.

**1.9** Runions house, Seattle, 1972: exterior. Ralph Anderson, architect.

Northwest School and a pioneer in historic preservation. Anderson's designs are in many ways similar to Zema's, but Anderson's firm was much larger and his work inevitably bore a less personal impress (fig. 1.9). The office was a training ground for many young Seattle architects, among them James Olson, who in later years would be principal in Olson/Walker (then Olson Sundberg and Olson Sundberg Kundig Allen, now Olson Kundig). Olson and Suyama had been friends in college years, and remained so. Olson remembers that every Friday afternoon the Anderson office had a big party, a manifestation of the office's "bohemian lifestyle," but this was "mixed with a very serious concern about design, within the realm of the Northwest palette—wood, expressing the structure, attention to site." And there was, too, as at Zema's office, a Japanese influence; Olson notes that "it was in all of us in that generation," but "with George it was especially strong." Equally important was the frequent presence of Jean Jongeward, an interior designer of

exceptional talent, who worked with Anderson on many projects, and imbued in Suyama an abiding respect for that profession at a time when such respect was not widespread among architectural offices.[9]

George stayed with the Anderson office for nearly three years, leaving in late 1970 to work, briefly, for Harris, Reed, and Litzenberger in Tacoma. At about the same time, at a party at the Richard White Gallery, Jim Olson introduced George to Kim Hewitt. Kim is a native of Tacoma, had obtained a degree in history from Whitman College in Walla Walla, but she had no background in architecture other than a brief exposure to its history in Whitman's freshman survey program. She would soon be working as secretary to the budget manager for King County, and shortly would advance to the role of budget analyst for the county, then for Seattle Public Schools. She was hosting her parents at dinner that evening; they invited Jim and George to join them. Although Kim was "a bit annoyed" at the inclusion of unexpected (and uncooked-for) guests,

she found that her "very particular cat liked George right away," and so did she. After dating for several months, Kim and George were married on April 17, 1971; George's father generously financed a honeymoon in San Francisco and the California coast. Did Kim see in George indications of remarkable future success? "I never thought about it; it didn't matter; I was happy to be with him on whatever path he chose to follow." George acknowledges that her stable income allowed him to begin his own practice. He did so immediately.

He worked from home for several months, then, for a year, claimed a desk in Jim Olson's office in the Pioneer Square district of Seattle's old downtown. In February 1973, he found "an old shack" at Eastlake Avenue and Newton Street, almost opposite Zema's office, with a "fabulous view" from a roof deck. Using salvaged materials, he made the shack and its roof deck into an office. In 1978 he drew Ric Peterson into the practice. Peterson's pragmatic and analytical way of working was valuable as a complement to Suyama's emphasis on the artistic and his reliance on intuition. Peterson became a full partner in the firm in 1983, but he remembers the early years of their time together as "the good days."

In the decade from 1973 through 1982, Suyama designed eleven residences and twenty-six remodels, including two condominiums and four residential additions. Many other projects, however, were mundane—the file log of those years is characterized by project descriptions such as "deck," "garage," "kitchen," "triplex," "alterations," "bathroom," "stair," "detail work shop," and most desperate of all, "employee shower" and "garage move." Suyama was trying to keep bread on the table in an economically depressed time, in a city overpopulated with architects. Nevertheless, he was becoming increasingly known for his mastery of design in wood, in an idiom similar to that of Anderson and Zema. The 1979 remodeling of Tom and Ethel Garside's home is representative of his best work of that period (fig. 1.10). Through such projects he continued to enlarge his circle of friends. One friend was Drake Salladay, owner of the open-air Pike Place Flowers shop in the Pike Place Market, for whom Suyama designed a second shop; Salladay was instrumental

**1.11** House for George and Kim Suyama, 1917 Broadway Avenue East, Seattle, 1979: interior. George Suyama, architect.

**1.12** 1979 Suyama house: interior.

in introducing Suyama to a client of major importance to his career (see chapter 2).

In those early years, George and Kim also remodeled four houses for themselves, the sale of each renovation financing the next, with a bit of profit left over. In those remodelings, George was most able to pursue his design ambitions. That work was also receiving some publicity. One of the houses, in Seattle's Madison Park, was featured in the *Seattle Times Pictorial* and was mentioned on three occasions in *Sunset* magazine, widely read on the West Coast.[10] Their home on Broadway Avenue East, which George began remodeling in 1979, was published in March of 1982 in the less widely read but prestigious *Architectural Digest* (figs. 1.11 and 1.12).

In 1977 George and Kim went to Europe for the first time, traveling for six weeks in France, Italy, Greece, and Crete. Mont Saint-Michel and the Greek temples remain George's dominant architectural memories; "architecture of ostentation or spectacle—Versailles, the Coliseum—was not very interesting to me." Kim notes, however, that most of his photographs from that trip were not of buildings at all, but of "the rich coherent urban fabric—walkways by canals, intimate spaces, all the little details—doors, foodstalls, shops, markets—I think he was absorb-

ing and recording what he saw as a different way of living." George's dearest memory of the trip is of the landscape experiences of a day on Crete, the lovely, sun-swept setting of the Palace of Minos in the hills above Iraklion, and their hotel room in the harbor that evening, whose french doors opened to a terrace twenty feet from the Mediterranean shore. George was responding to environmental experiences rather than architectural objects.

George maintained his friendship with Gene Zema during those years; they shared frequent lunches, and George accompanied Gene to nurseries to buy plants that Gene would develop as bonsai specimens. George and Kim joined the Zemas' tennis club. And George and Gene considered a business partnership. By 1976 Gene had largely given up the design and construction of buildings for others, and as early as 1968 he had converted the Eastlake office into a showroom. From his long-standing interest in and study of Japanese antiquities, he had become an authority in the field and was building a successful business by acquiring artifacts on commission and for retail. In 1979, George and Gene traveled together in Japan, where, with Gene's expert guidance, George first saw Japan's traditional buildings and their settings at first hand. They visited Himeji Castle (fig. 1.13), the Shinto shrine buildings of

Ise (fig. 1.14), the Kasuga shrine and the Todai-ji in Nara (fig. 1.15), the Katsura villa and the Ginkaku-ji, Ryoan-ji, and Kiyomizu-dera temples (fig. 1.16) in and around Kyoto, and the thatched-roof *gazzho-zukuri minkas* (farmhouses) in Takayama. Through these experiences, for which Zema's architecture and his collection of artifacts were only a modest preparation, George discovered "an incredible fondness for the Japanese aesthetic of arts and crafts—the reverence for nature—the intimate relationship, the complete integration, of building and garden. I had grown up in a Europe-oriented country, and many in my community, if asked whether they wanted to be Japanese, would have said 'no.' So I had had no preparation for this aesthetic immersion. It was new to me, and it seemed extraordinarily important."

The early years of Suyama's practice, however, had been ones of increasing challenge to the essentially modernist tenets that governed his work and his beliefs. Louis I. Kahn had emerged as a superb teacher at the University of Pennsylvania and as an architect whose work com- manded universal respect. His 1972 library for Philips Exeter Academy in Exeter, New Hampshire; the Kimbell Museum in Fort Worth, completed in the same year; and the Yale Center for British Art, which opened in 1977, remain as majestic examples of his extraordinary talent, and his renown was undiminished by his death in 1973. Fame notwithstanding, his work stood largely alone, as had Frank Lloyd Wright's in the pre- vious generation.[11] The controversies in architectural theory that had beset Suyama's late college years had coalesced into Contextualism, Postmodernism, and New Classicism, and those movements domi- nated architectural discourse in the late 1970s and the early 1980s. New Classicism was championed by Alan Greenberg, who persuasively argued that modernism had gone astray in rejecting historically based forms, that the Greco-Roman way of building in particular, having left a lasting language of architecture for the western world, should usefully persist. That movement, nevertheless, did not achieve widespread influ- ence, and it was little felt in the Pacific Northwest.

Postmodernism was a different matter. In the late 1970s, the Seattle Art Museum intended to build, on a site on First Avenue in downtown Seattle, an urban complement to its Moderne–Art Deco building of 1931–33 in the more pastoral Volunteer Park. Robert Venturi, whose *Complexity and Contradiction in Architecture* had been postmodernism's first architectural manifesto, was given the commission; the new building was scheduled to open in 1981. Venturi was designing the Sainsbury Wing of the National Gallery in London at the same time,[12] and it was largely on that basis that he was commissioned for the Seattle

project—but few expected that the new SAM would so closely emulate the Sainsbury Wing. The Sainsbury's eroded corner reappeared in the Seattle scheme, with no comparable reason for its existence, and the Sainsbury's great stairway reappeared too, in the same location and in only slightly different décor, at the expense of badly needed gallery space on the constrained site. The museum's entry stair from Second Avenue, which was meant to be a wry comment on the mundane, could indeed be mistaken for the mundane. Farther south, in Portland, Oregon, Michael Graves's Portland Building was being built at about the same time, to open in 1982. Widely publicized as the definitive icon of postmodernism even before its construction, it too revealed some all-too-evident flaws, particularly in the claustrophobic working floors whose windows, determined by Graves's pseudo-Classic façades, bore no relationship to interior needs.

In those same years, the preservation movement, energized by an increasing hostility to modernism and intensified by the 1964 demolition of New York's Pennsylvania Station, claimed major victories in Seattle's 1974 watershed preservation of its Pike Place Market, and the subsequent widespread restoration of buildings there and in Pioneer Square. Both districts were early recipients of Historic District designation. The Harvard/Belmont district and the Columbia City neighborhood would follow.

Preservation excepted, Suyama was not drawn into any of these movements. He read the major literature on postmodernism, an experience that, Kim recalls, was "difficult for George; it made him question himself a lot." In the end he found it, and its associated movements, unconvincing; they seemed to him superficial, even trivial, when compared to his own reliance on space, structure, materials, and, increasingly, site. Partner Ric Peterson characterizes Suyama as "continuously and intensely self-critical, never satisfied," and Kim sees him as "a perfectionist, his own toughest critic, constantly searching." Suyama had been for some time dissatisfied with the mode of his work. He was seeking growth and change within his own terms.

1. Unless noted otherwise, all personal information in this book is from conversations between the author and the referenced parties.

2. No substantial remains of the camp survive. Although the camp bore the name of the tiny town of Minidoka, the two bore no geographic relationship to one another.

3. George Nakashima, a 1939 graduate of the University of Washington's architecture program, was interned at the same camp, where, ironically, he learned the Japanese craft of furniture making, for which he would achieve renown, from fellow internee Gentaro Hikogawa. Nakashima was released in 1943 because of the intervention of architect Antonin Raymond. Among many other honors, Nakashima was recognized, on June 8, 1990, as the university's Summa Laude Dignatus, the highest honor the university confers; he died a week later.

4. Jane Jacobs, *The Death and Life of Great American Cities* (New York: Random House, 1993; originally published 1961).

5. Robert Venturi, *Complexity and Contradiction in Architecture* (New York: Museum of Modern Art, 1966).

6. For more on Pries, see Jeffrey Karl Ochsner, *Lionel H. Pries, Architect, Artist, Educator* (Seattle and London: University of Washington Press, 2007). Ochsner makes a convincing case that Pries should be ranked with Eliel Saarinen, W. R. B. Wilcox, and Paul Philippe Cret, as one of the most influential architectural educators of the 1930s.

7. The degree was soon to change to a four-year, undergraduate, nonprofessional degree entitled Bachelor of Arts in Environmental Design, or BAED. The BAED was intended to be followed by a new professional-entry degree, the Master of Architecture, which had been used theretofore for extended study in design or research following on the professional Bachelor of Architecture. These changes were not universally applauded; they added yet another layer to the confusion of programs at Washington and elsewhere.

8. Daniel M. Streissguth, faculty member and, at the time, chair of the Department of Architecture, was originally selected as architect for the building. Given the scale of the work, he drew Zema into the project as full partner, and three other architects as associates: Dale Benedict, Claus Seligmann, and myself.

9. The meager respect was based in part on the dominance of architects in the field of furniture design at that time. That was the era of Eero Saarinen's Womb Chair and his Pedestal series, Harry Bertoia's pressed steel mesh chairs, Isamu Noguchi's free-form, glass-topped coffee table, and the many designs by Ray and Charles Eames. It was also the era of the great Nordic furniture designers: in Denmark, Hans Wegner, Finn Juhl, and Borge Mogensen; and in Sweden, Bruno Mathsson, Carl Malmsten, and Yngve Ekström. Although designed much earlier, Mies van der Rohe's many furniture pieces, and an equal number by Marcel Breuer, were being produced in the United States by Knoll, and Alvar Aalto's timeless designs, dating mostly from earlier decades, were also available. In part, too, the lack of respect for interior designers was based in the architects' evangelical passion for modernism, a passion less intensely felt in the interiors field. The hostility was occasionally blatant, as in Frank Lloyd Wright's endlessly repeated reference to "inferior desecrators."

10. *Seattle Times Pictorial*, November 10, 1974, pp. 44–55; and *Sunset*, May 1975, December 1975, and October 1979.

11. In the mid-1970s, Romaldo Giurgola, who in some respects might be considered Kahn's protégé, designed the new law school building, Condon Hall, for the University of Washington. A few years later Giurgola proposed for the Seattle Art Museum a building that would remain unbuilt, for the site ultimately occupied by the Westlake Center.

12. That Venturi was chosen for the London project was in part a consequence of Prince Charles's outcry against modernism, which had led to the rejection of an earlier scheme. Venturi's readiness to address the question of the new Sainsbury Wing's relationship to the existing National Gallery, and his remarkably adept management of that relationship, yielded a design that has generally met with high praise.

# 2

Evolution

In 1982 Suyama began construction of a new office for his practice at 121 East Boston Street, on the southeast corner of its intersection with Yale Avenue, a block west of Gene Zema's office. The property extended eastward to Eastlake, and included an existing one-story, brick commercial building from the 1920s, fronting on Eastlake, that would become the Serafina Restaurant. Between it and the new office, Suyama created a courtyard (fig. 2.1) to serve both office and restaurant, accessed from the west side of the restaurant and, from Boston Street, by means of a stair and a gate integrated with the new office. The exterior of the complex, and especially the north elevation with courtyard wall and gate (fig. 2.2), makes a strikingly sympathetic contribution to the ambience of the neighborhood. Suyama moved his practice into the new building in early 1983 (fig. 2.3), at which time Ric Peterson became a full partner in the firm.

## THE BENAROYA CONDOMINIUM

In that same year, Jack and Rebecca Benaroya bought an unfinished loft condominium space on Seattle's First Hill. Although some spatial divisions are needed in any habitable residence, the Benaroyas wanted to retain the loft's magnificent views to Elliott Bay, Lake Union, and Lake Washington, and to the distant Cascade mountain range to the east and the Olympics on the western horizon. They commissioned a competition among several Seattle architects to propose designs for the interior. Suyama's work was not sufficiently well known at that time, or sufficiently remarkable in itself, to have drawn him to the attention of the Benaroyas, but when Drake Salladay, for whom Suyama had designed a complement to Salladay's open-air flower shop at the Pike Place Market, recommended him to them, the Benaroyas included him among the competitors. His proposal was selected from the three submitted.

The building's fixed elements—structural columns, mechanical and electrical shafts, fire stairs, and elevators—were organized in two central service cores flanking the elevator lobby. Suyama's design encloses the service cores within a family of dramatically curved walls, unusual in his work, that echo the given curved corners of the building, and ease some room-to-room transitions. Subordinate spaces—baths, closets, kitchen—are configured within and around these walls. The column-free space between these elements and the exterior walls is quite freely organized into various zones for seating and dining. The

2.1 Suyama's Boston Street office, Seattle, 1982–83: the courtyard, looking northeast. George Suyama, architect.

2.2 Suyama's 1982–83 office: the north entry to the courtyard.

2.3 Suyama's 1982–83 office: the interior.

novel feature of Suyama's proposal, however, was a system of opaque movable wall panels—the Japanese term would be *fusuma*—that could slide perpendicular to the exterior walls, or pivot against them or the interior fixed walls, to modify the major living spaces in almost infinite variety (figs. 2.4 and 2.5). The panels were to be of high-density particle board, finished with thirty coats of subtly transparent lacquer, each coat hand-rubbed. As the design developed, the panels became a more minor element of the interior—there are only six of them in the final design—

and by and large they have remained in relatively fixed locations. But they led Suyama into a new way of thinking about walls, and a generous budget allowed him to explore highly refined details. For these reasons he regards this project as "a watershed," although the full realization of its influence would only evolve over time. Furnishings were fabricated by Kurt Beardslee, working in coordination with Suyama, interior designer Terry Hunziker, and the client.

**2.4** Condominium interior for Jack and Rebecca Benaroya, Seattle, 1983: looking toward the major living space; a movable panel is at center. George Suyama, architect.

**2.5** Benaroya condominium: the living space, with the breakfast area beyond and other movable panels at center.

Two years later George and Kim went to Egypt with Jim and Katherine Olson. They visited Cairo, the Giza pyramid field, and the Abu Simbel temples, and went by boat down the Nile to Luxor. George had an immediate empathy for "the ancient elemental forms, austere, primal, precisely declared," but he was equally intrigued by the intimate folk art objects in the Cairo Museum. Four years later he would find a similar enthusiasm for the site, and the exquisite masonry, of Machu Picchu.

## THE FIRST FAUNTLEROY HOUSE, "FAUNTLEROY I"

In 1986 Suyama began work on yet another home for himself and Kim, the first that he would design in its entirety. He says that the house was a conscious homage to Gene Zema, as several later projects would be. The site is on the shore of a shallow cove of the West Seattle shoreline, in the neighborhood known as Fauntleroy, just north of the dock that serves the ferry to Vashon Island. The street is to the east; westward is a dramatic view across the sound to Vashon and Bainbridge Islands, with

**2.6** The first house on the Fauntleroy cove for George and Kim Suyama ("Fauntleroy I"), Seattle, 1986: the house and its neighbors, from the shore. George Suyama, architect.

**2.7** Fauntleroy I: plan.

**2.8** Fauntleroy I: section.

SECOND FLOOR PLAN

FIRST FLOOR PLAN

N

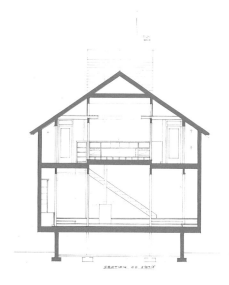

SECTION CC

the Olympic Mountains on the horizon. Because of the locations of existing houses along the shore, it was possible here to build closer to the water's edge than would normally be allowed (fig. 2.6). The site drops sharply at its east-west mid-point, from an elevation roughly that of the street to a plateau not much above high tide; the change in elevation is accommodated within the length of the garage.

The plan includes, at the upper level, the garage, an entry reached by a bridge, a master and a guest bedroom, and a small bath with shower and Japanese tub (fig. 2.7). A stair at the center of the plan leads downward to the lower floor, which merges with the lower plateau of the site (figs. 2.7 and 2.9). The lower level includes an "entry" at the foot of the stair, a dining space, a shop under the garage, and, at a slightly lower floor level, a living space. A deck, spanned by the entry bridge, claims the space between the garage and the house and serves the dining space; another deck opens to the shore from the living space (fig. 2.10).

**2.9** Fauntleroy I: elevations.

**2.10** Fauntleroy I: from the shore.

**2.11** Fauntleroy I: the living space. The exposed structure establishes
multiple scales, to tops of doors, bottoms of beams, and the ceiling plane.

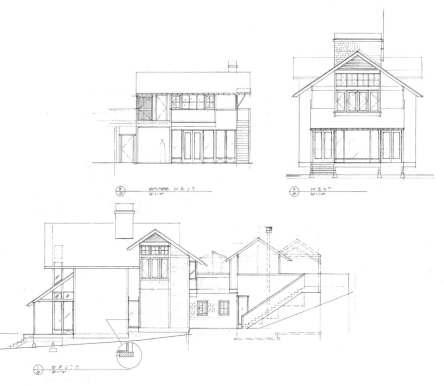

Wood is the dominant material—inside and out, and, as is typical of Zema's work, the wood structure is the organizing element of much of the plan, establishing five bays symmetrically about the east-west centerline, with a similar order of north-to-south bays. Much of the wood structure is evident to the eye, as is again typical of Zema: the roof beams and rafter tails are visible on the exterior, projecting beyond the edges of the deep overhangs. In the interior, the major beams are exposed on both floors, and the second-floor joists are expressed in the battens of the lower floor ceiling (fig. 2.11). Another reflection of Zema's work are the many columns within or outside the major spaces, rather than within the walls, that create implied subspaces, while the actual wall-to-wall dimensions can be maximized within a small house. The detailing of each structural intersection is developed with an elegant complexity that at the same time shows rigorous logic in its making. The Benaroya sliding panels reappear as space modifiers; one can be slid across the *tansu* chest of figure 2.11 to reveal the television and sound system; another reveals or conceals Kim's piano. Much of the cabinetwork and several furniture pieces are by Dale Brotherton.

2.12 Condominium interior for Bruce Nordstrom, 1986: the fireplace. George Suyama, architect.

2.13 The Nordstrom condominium: the view to a terrace; the Seattle skyline beyond.

2.14 The Nordstrom condominium: view up a column.

## THE NORDSTROM CONDOMINIUM

In 1986 George began another condominium interior, this one for Bruce Nordstrom. Unlike the Benaroyas' building, the pragmatic elements of Nordstrom's building, also in Seattle, are not organized into two cores; rather the vertical air distribution ducts and electrical shafts are clustered around individual structural columns in a grid of fairly regular bays. Suyama has housed each cluster of column, ducts, and shafts in what, to the eye, seems to be a family of four robust wooden columns (figs. 2.13 and 2.14). These in turn carry paired wooden beams in both cardinal directions and support the wooden ceiling that masks the concrete ceiling slab and provides a means for air distribution. The detailing of the wooden elements, however, is unlike that of Suyama's Fauntleroy house. The crisp crafting suggests a more meticulous reprise of the interior of Himeji, or an Ise built of rectangular rather than cylindrical elements (fig. 2.14). Suyama acknowledges that those associations are evident, as they will be in varying degrees in his work from this time onward, but he believes they arose subconsciously, without overt intention. Kurt Beardslee was again the designer and fabricator of many of the furnishings, but in this case he was assisted by a young metalworker, David Gulassa, who had been inspired by Beardslee's work. Gulassa built the bronze basin in the Nordstrom powder room.

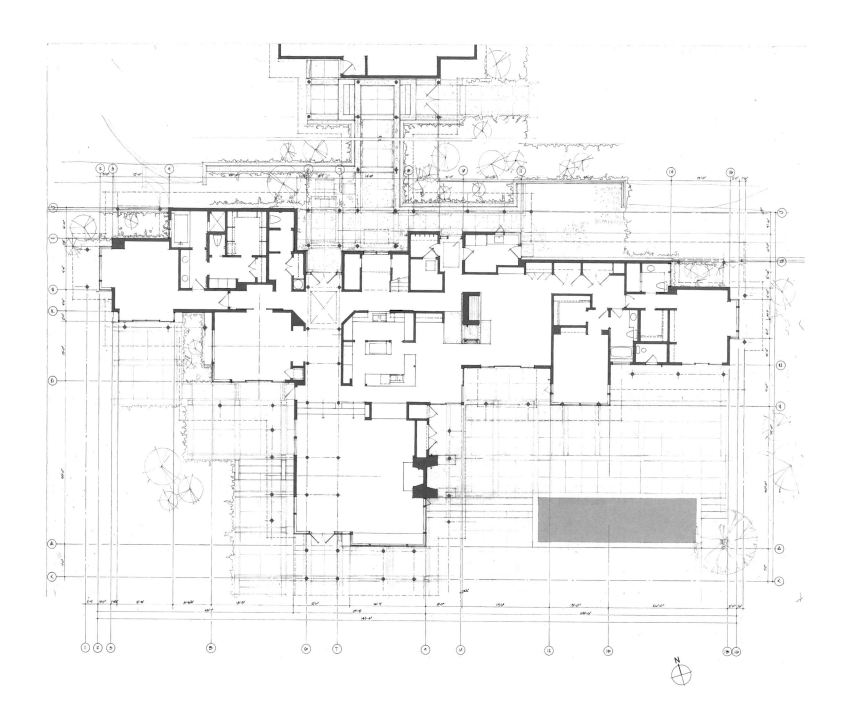

**2.15** House for Jim and Carolyn Milgard, Allen Point, near Gig Harbor, WA, 1986–87: plan. George Suyama, architect.

**2.16** The Milgard house: the entry pergola.

**2.17** House for Donald and Sylvia Campbell, Vancouver, WA, 1989–92: the exterior from the south. George Suyama, architect.

## THE MILGARD HOUSE

The elevations of the house for Jim and Carolyn Milgard of 1987, as shown on an exquisite contract drawing (fig. 2.15), again reflect an influence from Gene Zema. Yet the axially extended colonnade also suggests a Japanese influence—the repeated bays recall the Fushimi Inari shrine near Kyoto, as the round columns equally recall Ise (fig. 2.16). As Suyama remembers the evolution of the design, the colonnade arose from an intrinsic desire to emphasize the waterfront orientation. The property is on Allen Point near Gig Harbor, in the convoluted southwest-

ern reaches of Puget Sound. The round columns, on the other hand, and the light maple finish of the woodwork, were a response to the client's wish for a somewhat more traditional ambience.

## THE CAMPBELL HOUSE

The house for Don and Sylvia Campbell of 1989–90, in Vancouver, Washington, is the largest and last of Suyama's Zema-inspired projects (fig. 2.17). It includes a courtyard that one must traverse to reach

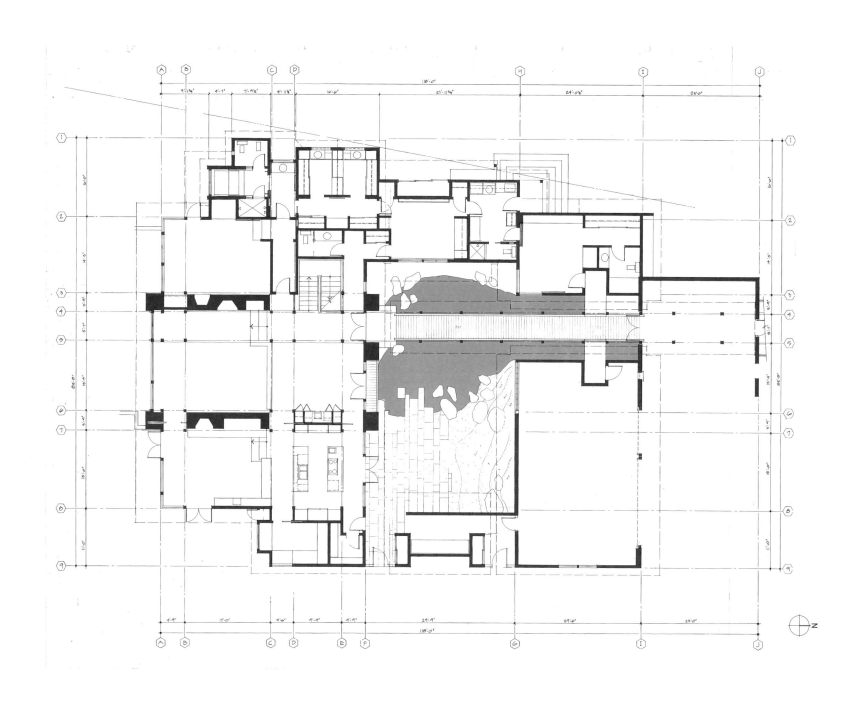

**2.18** The Campbell house: plan.

**2.19** The Campbell house: the pergola.

**2.20** The Campbell house: the interior near the entry, with the battened sloped ceiling over the lateral bay.

the entry to the house proper. (This compositional theme, which will appear again in Suyama's work, evokes the entry sequence of Zema's house on Whidbey Island, designed in about 1986; see fig. 1.5.) The Campbell courtyard is bisected by a pergola whose columns establish a spatial and structural spine that continues throughout the length of the plan, and around which the entire composition develops (figs. 2.18 and 2.19). The visual drama of the structural system, of which the spine is a part, works in concert with a complex spatial drama that is a sig-

nificant elaboration of that in Suyama's own house. As one enters from the Campbell pergola along the edge of the dining room, the door heads and the bottoms of the beams are again an intimate seven feet above the floor, but above the beams the ceiling rises as a sloped battened plane (fig. 2.20).

As one moves to the second interior bay of the spine, the ceiling is a horizontal plane eight and a half feet from the floor, suspended from secondary structural elements above the still-low major beams.

**2.21** The Campbell house: the stair looking toward the entry.

**2.22** The Campbell house: the living room looking toward the dining space. At upper right can be seen the three layers of beams, each of which plays its own role in physical support, spatial organization, and formal articulation.

In the next bay, a cross-axial skylight rises to bring a flood of light into the edges of the dining space, the kitchen, and the living and family rooms beyond. Then, in the living space, the family room, and the master bedroom, the floor plane descends another eighteen inches, thereby increasing the ceiling height to ten feet; and because of the treatment of the preceding spaces, these major spaces are felt to be appropriately grand in vertical dimension (fig. 2.22).

**2.23** The William Traver Gallery, Seattle, 1991: as seen from the gallery. George Suyama, architect.

**2.24** The Traver Gallery: the reception area.

## THE WILLIAM TRAVER GALLERY

In association with Knute Hanson, in 1991 Suyama designed a new provision for the William Traver Gallery in the historically significant Paulsen Building on First Avenue, a block north of the Seattle Art Museum.[1] Suyama had known Traver for several years, and both client and architect envisioned the new gallery as a space with its own architectural presence. The separation of structure and wall planes at the entry presages much of Suyama's subsequent work, and the resultant transparent corner provides a dramatic view into the gallery and its displayed material (fig. 2.23), while the steel and wood reception desk by David

Gulassa is a striking work of art in its own right (fig. 2.24). Much of the necessarily neutral display space can be arranged to suit the needs of the immediate exhibits by means of sliding and pivoting panels on barn-door tracks that are progeny of the Benaroya panels.

## THE KEMPER RETREAT

In 1986 Kraig and Kathy Kemper bought an irregular forty-acre site in Skagit County, adjacent to the Pioneer Bay View Cemetery to the south and overlooking, directly to the west, the Padilla Bay National Estuaries

**2.25** The Kraig and Kathy Kemper cabin, 1992–95: from the west.
George Suyama, architect.

Research Reserve, a nursery for fish and crab and for the kelp beds used by the Brant Geese. Beyond the Reserve, the coastal town of Anacortes can be seen and, beyond Anacortes, thirteen of the San Juan Islands; Lummi Island is visible to the northwest. The Kempers camped on the site for a few years, during which they became increasingly immersed in the natural history of the area. They were avid observers of the deer, opossum, raccoons, and "plethora of birds" that breed on the site in the spring; Kraig served on the board of the Washington Ornithological Society and was president of Skagit Audubon. When in 1992 the Kempers decided to build a durable shelter on the site, their foremost criterion was that it not foreclose the immediate sensory awareness of nature—its sounds and smells, its humidity and temperature—that was the essential value of the place.

Kraig Kemper, a landscape architect, had spent three months in Japan studying Japanese gardens and had worked with Tom Kubota on Seattle's renowned Kubota Gardens. Kraig had also worked with George Suyama on a number of jobs over the years. He "always knew" that someday he would choose Suyama for an architectural project, "because of his wood detailing,"[2] and also, perhaps, because Kraig knew that George envisioned a similar kind of environment for Kim and himself.

The choice location on the site, looking toward Lummi Island, was deliberately rejected for the shelter, since once built upon, it would no longer exist in its natural state. Kraig and George decided that the shelter should be immediately to the north. In this they were influenced by the Tokugawa shrine at Nikko, whose buildings avoid, and thereby preserve, the choice site locations of the mountainside.

Suyama's earliest conceptual sketch was of a tent floating above the land—he spoke of the building as a "permanent tent"—and the overall configuration is tentlike in its rectangular plan and its single gable roof (fig. 2.25). Early on the decision was made to make the building an exercise in wood, most of it western red cedar. Kemper would be the general contractor, Dale Brotherton the craftsman/builder. Brotherton had trained with a Japanese carpenter in California, then gone to Japan to work directly under a Japanese carpenter. Kraig knew of Brotherton's career, and George had used Brotherton's extraordinary abilities on

**2.26** The Kemper cabin: detail.

**2.27** The Kemper cabin: axonometric exploded view.

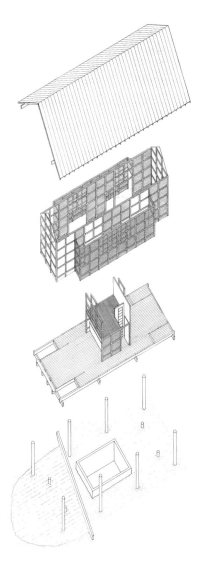

other projects, including his own Fauntleroy house. No nails, screws, or bolts would be used for the shelter's wood connections. All surfaces were to be hand-planed to a finished surface, without sanding—a technique requiring extraordinary skill, since the blade of the plane can easily catch in the grain and penetrate the surface of the piece, thereby destroying its dimension and planarity. The columns at the eaves, however, which are the major structural support, are of concrete, and the structure is laterally stabilized by stainless steel cables (fig. 2.26).

The plan, except for the two-story center element, seems not unlike that of Mies van der Rohe's Farnsworth house in Plano, Illinois, built in 1958. Spatially and experientially, the Kemper shelter is quite different (fig. 2.27). Circulation is by means of autonomous screened galleries on the north and south flanks. One must enter these to move from any one space to another, and since they lie on the outboard edges

2.28 The Kemper cabin: the southern gallery and the sleeping room, with the rising land of the woods in the distance.

2.29 The Kemper cabin: the great room, looking from the sleeping loft toward the shore and the islands.

2.30 The Kemper cabin: the great room, looking east toward the kitchen and the loft above.

2.31 The Kemper cabin: the sleeping room, the northern gallery, and the edge of the woods.

of the building, they bring an insistent intimate integration with the trees, the earth, the birds (fig. 2.28). Sliding panels, gliding on barn-door tracks, open or close the galleries to the spaces between. The seaward of these spaces, which the Kempers call the "Great Room," is twenty feet from floor to ridge, and its height, breadth, and length are a dramatic contrast to the intimacy of the galleries (fig. 2.29). The Great Room is strongly axial in its plan dimensions and in the configuration of its roof; it seems to reach toward the falling meadowland to the north-west and to the sound and the San Juan Islands beyond.

Slightly east of the midpoint of the building, a two-story element provides bath and storage below and a loft space above. The Kempers sleep in the loft on winter days because what heat there is in the little building is concentrated there. The main sleeping space comprises the landward third of the structure's main level; it looks toward rising land and the near trees of the dense woods (figs. 2.28, 2.31).

In the course of the Kemper adventure, in 1993, Suyama was elected to the College of Fellows of the American Institute of Architects, for his record of excellence in design.

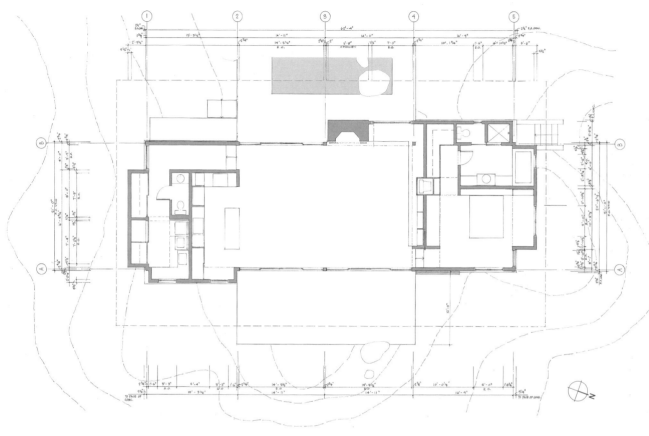

2.32 House for Jim and Christina Lockwood, Lopez Island, WA, 1996: from the south. George Suyama, architect.

2.33 The Lockwood house: plan.

2.34 The Lockwood house: the approach. The landscape as entry.

## THE LOCKWOOD HOUSE

The house for Jim and Christina Lockwood on Lopez Island, designed and built in 1996, is the last of Suyama's major projects in which a wood structure governs the design; it is also the first in which Bruce Hinckley was involved as landscape architect (fig. 2.32).

Hinckley is a Seattle native, a graduate of the Lakeside School, who after undergraduate study at Brigham Young University received a master's degree in landscape architecture from Utah State University. He maintains offices under the firm name "Alchemie" in Seattle;

Ketchum, Idaho; and, until recently, Vancouver, British Columbia. His work has appeared in many books and distinguished journals and has received many design awards. He and Suyama have found that their views on architecture and landscape are uniquely complementary. The Lockwood project was the first of many in which they have been professional associates. They have also become close personal friends.

The Lockwood design includes a main house and a guest house, flanking a terrace to which the two structures are axially and almost

2.35 The Lockwood house: the living pavilion.

**2.36** The Lockwood house: the northwest corner of the living space.

**2.37** The Lockwood house: the tokonoma.

symmetrically related (fig. 2.33). The interior spaces of the two build-ings are still gathered within single boundaries, whose walls serve as supporting structures for the two roofs. But the roofs, both of them pure rectangles with generous overhangs, have begun to declare themselves as independent sheltering planes.

The site was regarded as being itself the entry. One climbs a rocky declivity, a natural gateway, to arrive at the paved court with its pool (fig. 2.34), from which the main house opens seaward; while the guest house, at a slightly higher elevation, is withdrawn into the woods. The main house is primarily a pavilion whose glass walls open on one side to the court, with its reflecting pool, and opposite, to an eastern ter-race, with a majestic view to the Strait of Juan de Fuca (fig. 2.35). The landward northwest corner of the living room is developed as a snug haven: the fireplace hearth extends to the right of the fireplace as the floor of a recess, a room within a room, with its own autonomous low ceiling and a small window looking out to the pool (fig. 2.36). The hearth/floor and a vestige of the lower ceiling then turn the corner to create a subspace evoking a tokonoma, then both continue—the ceiling vestige as a lighting cove above the bookshelves, the hearth/elevated floor as a cantilevered seat or shelf below (fig. 2.37). The bedroom and the kitchen at either end of the pavilion likewise are treated as refuges, with largely opaque walls and minimal dimensions.

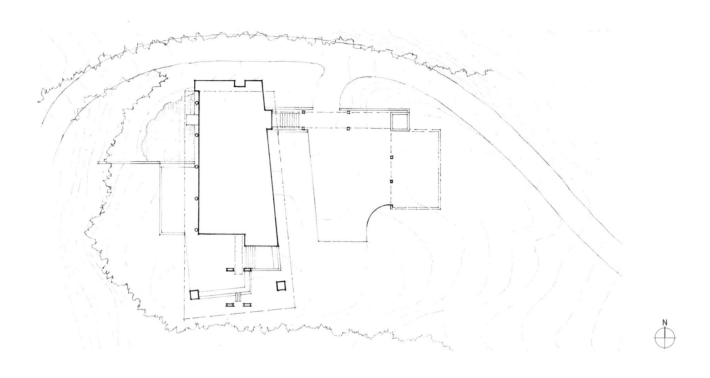

## THE MARTIN PROJECT

The project for a house for Thomas Martin came to the office in 1990. The drama of its design would mean that the bid figures were far over budget and it would remain unbuilt, but it is the clearest evidence of the direction in which Suyama's thoughts were moving at this time. He is quick to acknowledge that John Fleming, who had several years' experience with Albuquerque architect Antoine Predock,[3] was the primary designer for the project. Fleming brought to Suyama's office "a dialectic of intellectual introspection at a time when we embraced that significance."

The Martins' site had been used for Native American potlatches, and the cross-axial organization of the house is intended to reference the cross-axes of the typical native longhouse (fig. 2.38). The Martin scheme comprises a number of spatial and formal elements on two floors, each of complex but clear rectilinear geometry, all under a trapezoidal roof, with one doubly curved surface supported by a line of columns to the west, bearing walls to the east, and a double range of pylons along the north-south axis. The pylons grasp a catwalk-like corridor that accesses the three second-floor bedrooms (figs. 2.39, 2.40, 2.41).

One would have entered through an attenuated colonnade-like space—the east-west axis—not unlike that created by the colonnades of the Milgard and Campbell houses. This axial path would have led to a window and a small deck beyond, looking over falling land to the distant water. Before one had reached the window, however, the north-south axial path would have opened at left, presenting a view through five pairs of pylons, under the long catwalk. After two bays were traversed, the living room would open at right, with its view out to, again,

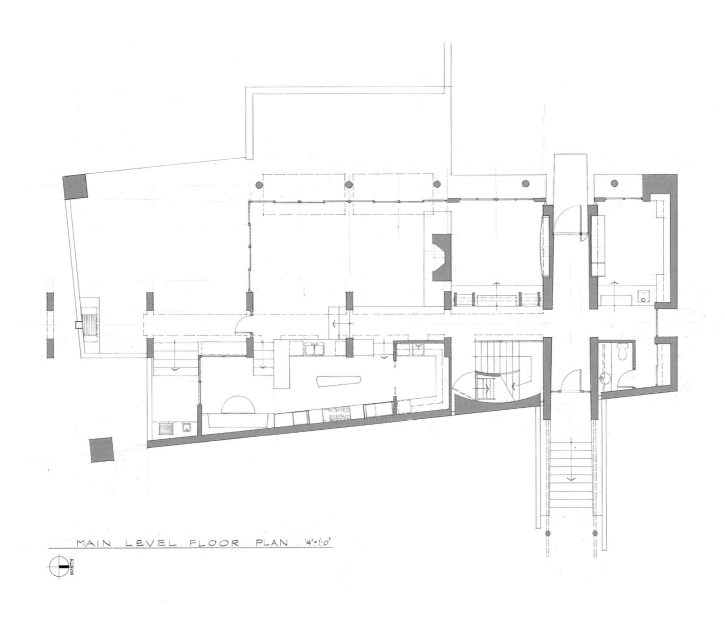

MAIN LEVEL FLOOR PLAN ¼"=1'-0"

NORTH

**2.38** House for Thomas Martin (1990; unbuilt): site plan. Suyama Architects;
John Fleming, project architect.

**2.39** The Martin project: main floor plan.

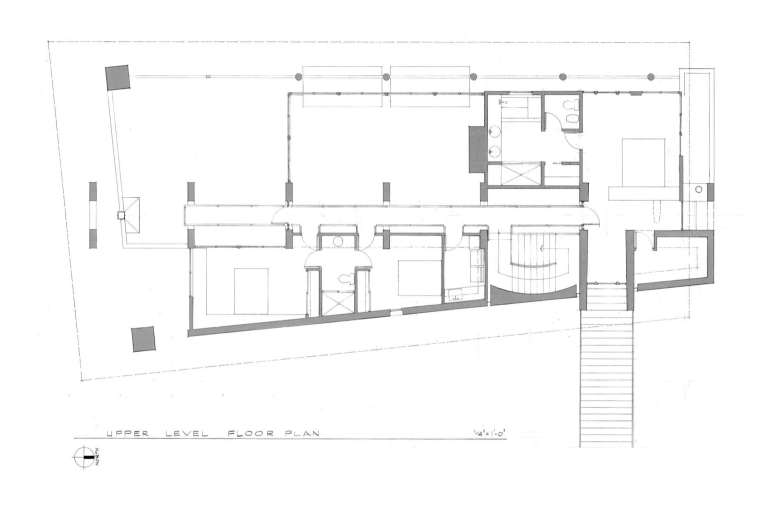

UPPER LEVEL FLOOR PLAN                    1/4"=1'-0"

NORTH

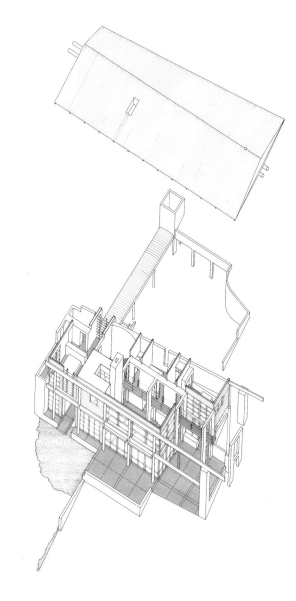

**2.40** The Martin project: upper floor plan.

**2.41** The Martin project: axonometric diagrammatic view.

the falling land and the distant water. The spatial sequence would have been much like that of Frank Lloyd Wright's Charles Ennis house in Los Angeles of 1920–24. In the spatial progression of the Martin design there would have been a sequence of scale changes as well: one would have moved from an entry with an eight-foot ceiling, past the dining room, whose lowered floor would have given it a ceiling height of eleven feet, to, finally, the living room, fully twenty-two feet in height.

To turn from an experiential analysis to a formal one, the solids of the Martin scheme can be seen to bear, throughout, ambiguous and multivalent relationships to the spaces, and to the evident axes as well. Wall masses seldom describe the spaces they bound; several of the most dramatic solids—those at the south end, for example—bear no relationship to spaces at all. The relatively simple roof gives no hint of the spatial and formal complexities it calmly gathers together. These

characteristics of the Martin design ally it with the avowed intentions of the Deconstruction movement that was then in its early stages, although Suyama had no such parallel in mind, and the coherent resolution of complex relationships in the Martin scheme is counter to deconstruction goals. The Martin scheme's ambiguities, complexities, and mutivalences, and its coherent resolutions thereof, had a large influence on Suyama's thought and work in the decade to follow.

1. Conversations with Kraig Kemper, December 2007.
2. With the enlargement of the Seattle Art Museum in 2006–7, the Traver Gallery is now directly across from the north end of the museum.
3. Predock was the 2006 recipient of the AIA Gold Medal, the highest honor the Institute confers; earlier recipients include Thomas Jefferson, Charles Follen McKim, Louis Sullivan, Frank Lloyd Wright, Le Corbusier, Alvar Aalto, and Louis I. Kahn; Glenn Murcutt was the recipient in 2009.

# 3

In the early years of the twenty-first century, George Suyama's work continued to take its direction from a simultaneous consideration of space, structure, and materials—the fundamental way of making architecture that he had long ago seen in Gene Zema's work—but the materials of choice changed, and with them the ways of managing both space and structure. Suyama describes his design work of this period as the manifestation of a sea change.

Although on the face of it, the sea change seems to have happened suddenly, it had actually been in gestation since at least 1983, when the Benaroya project led Suyama to a new way of thinking about walls—or perhaps suggested rethinking an old way, since the movable Benaroya panels may be seen as cousins to the traditional Japanese sliding *fusuma* screens. Likewise, the Nordstrom project of 1986 manifested, subconsciously or unconsciously, a Japaneseness of structure and materials quite different from the Zema idiom. Then the Martin project of 1990, which won a major award for unbuilt designs, jolted Suyama into a change of attitude toward his own ambitions. He believes, in retrospect, that the preponderance of mundane projects in his early professional years had lulled him into being too easily satisfied with

professional competence; the Martin project led him to think that he might reach toward more creative horizons. In this he acknowledges the crucial influence of its project architect, John Fleming. The Campbell house, completed in the year of the Martin project, is the last of the Zema-inspired designs. The Kemper bird-watching retreat of 1992 gave Suyama the opportunity to work out an overt Japanese influence, but that building would remain unique in his career.

Little in Suyama's sea change came from literature or theory. Although he still finds some difficulty with the printed word, he drove himself to read the many and lengthy architectural discourses of the 1980s and 1990s. He found them limited in their concerns, and therefore unconvincing; he notes the extraordinary predominance of ideas of allusion and metaphor in shaping the sculptural form of the building, and the nearly complete absence of any serious attention to the human experience within the architectural space. "Nothing in the then-current literature and thought satisfied me," he says. But he found adequate sources of growth and inspiration in the contributions and the talents of those who, in one way and another, had been brought into his projects. He is grateful to those others, and he readily acknowledges

3.1 Jay Deguchi, Ric Peterson, and George Suyama in the Second Avenue office.

their importance to his work; he refers to himself as the conductor of an orchestral performance, or "the catalyst within a Renaissance community."

Those important others include Ric Peterson, with Suyama since 1978. Suyama says, "Ric is the office's conscience. He holds things together; he is the rudder for the firm; he weighs the consequences of our actions and decisions." Jay Deguchi, who has been with the firm since 1992, has become a kindred spirit in design. Deguchi came to the office to learn to design in wood, for which Suyama was then renowned, yet, in the end, Deguchi imbued in the office his own predilection for steel and concrete, and his skill in their design. While Suyama continues to be governed by his intuitions—occasionally, he admits, his decisions are based on a simple whim—he believes that Deguchi has brought to the firm's design process "an innate intellectual logic." Suyama and Deguchi thus act as sounding boards for one another. "Jay brings something into my office and says 'What do you think of this?' And we have an easy exchange of ideas, with the goal of finding what is best for the project, what is the best product. Ego is secondary—Jay is a happy, gracious person, with no edge to get over; he balances Ric and me." In January 2002 Jay joined George and Ric as a full partner in the firm, which was renamed Suyama Peterson Deguchi (fig. 3.4).

Three designers outside the office have also been of crucial importance. With the Lockwood project of 1996, Suyama began a close and fruitful association with landscape architect Bruce Hinckley. Furniture maker Kurt Beardslee built the kitchen in Suyama's Madison Park house and many of the furnishings for the Benaroya and Nordstrom condominiums; George considers him a craftsman of "incredible importance; we connected on a philosophy of how one should live." Beardslee was also a mentor and an inspiration to David Gulassa, with whom Suyama increasingly worked as Beardslee left the field of furniture design to serve the cause of wildlife conservation. Gulassa was the fabricator of the basin in the Nordstrom condominium's powder room, whereby he led Suyama into the world of artistry in steel.

Gulassa had founded his own design and fabrication company in 1989, developing it into one of the region's premier design studios, with separate shops for metal, wood, and upholstery. His work was featured in *Architectural Digest* and the *New York Times*, and displayed in the Museum of Modern Art. Like Hinckley, Gulassa found inspiration in nature, in stones, driftwood, and leaves, but his more evident inspiration lay in the poetry of man-made things—the sculptural power of a ship's propeller, or the driving components of a steam engine. Gulassa, too, became George's professional kindred spirit, frequent project associate, and friend. Tragically, David Gulassa was killed in a boating accident on Lake Union in January of 2001. The Nordstrom project had offered Gulassa his first professional commission; Suyama says of him: "He was the practice of art and a work of art."[1]

Several projects discussed below reflect the changes in Suyama's thinking and orientation.

### THE SECOND AVENUE OFFICE

In 1997 Suyama Architects designed and occupied a new office at 2324 Second Avenue in the area of Seattle known as Belltown, half a dozen blocks north of the Pike Place Market. The building had been an auto repair shop. Suyama says of the remodeling, "minimal changes were made to the exterior or the building's original structure. A modest palette of drywall, steel, and plywood has transformed the interior, providing a contrast with the original structure while allowing the essence of its industrial origins to remain."[2] Nevertheless, those minimal exterior changes give the building a dramatic new street façade (fig. 3.2), and the interior is indeed transformed.

Immediately off the street are a small drafting room, at right, and, at left, "3 × 10," a retail accoutrements shop. Between these a steel-floored ramp ascends to a large high-ceilinged central space; this is what has become known as the "Suyama Space" (fig. 3.3, and see Appendix 1). Suyama has long been active in the Seattle arts community, and as an architect he admires, even envies, the artist's greater freedom. From the outset, Suyama Space has been dedicated to large-scale

art installations curated by Beth Sellars. Skylights introduced into the wood roof structure high above allow a modicum of natural light, and translucent walls at the north end encompass restrooms. Otherwise, this central space has been relatively little altered: the wood trusses that support the roof are as they have always been; the floor is the worn boards from days of car repair. A dramatic stairway from the street side of this space leads to a small conference room above. Opposite, beyond the art installation, are two floors of architectural offices. On the main floor are a drafting room, principals' offices, and a conference room (fig. 3.4). All are open to one another; surface materials are steel plates for floors, and the most inexpensive grade of plywood and gypsum

3.2 The new office at 2324 Second Avenue, Seattle, 1996–97; the streetfront. Suyama Architects.

3.3 Suyama Architects office: Suyama Space (prior to first installation in 1998).

3.4 Suyama Architects office: the work space.

plasterboard for cabinetwork and walls. Below, a basement provides a shop and model building space, a filing room, an area for coffee breaks, and limited parking.

Suyama says that designing the Second Avenue office was the greatest single influence on his change of direction in future works. There had been other influences as well, however, since this office, whose ambience is radically different from that of the Eastlake office, is itself evidence of a change of direction. Clearly Suyama regards the new office as part of the sea change in his work.

The new paradigm emerged also in an abundance of new work. In the early months of 1997, before the new office on Second Avenue was complete, Suyama was awarded an ostensibly residential commission whose great size demands a separate chapter (see chapter 4). In the same year, he began the design of the seminal Grevstad-Draheim retreat on Decatur Island. In 1997 Lyn and Gerald Grinstein returned to Seattle from Fort Worth, Texas, and the following year selected Suyama to design a large residence for them on the east shore of Lake Washington. Scott and Frances McAdams acquired a site on San Juan Island for which, in 1998, they asked Suyama to design a retreat; in that same year, he and Kim began thinking about a new house for themselves; and in 2003 Laurie and George Schuchart chose Suyama as architect for their new home in Broadmoor.

## THE GREVSTAD-DRAHEIM HOUSE

In 1997–98, Christian Grevstad and Terry Draheim owned a south-facing waterfront property on Decatur Island, one of the smaller of the San Juan Islands, accessed only by private boat or plane. A shallow declivity runs through the center of the site, north to south, the land dropping away gently, then more sharply, to a serpentine channel that wanders picturesquely among peninsular landforms. Suyama says the placement and design of the house consciously denies the view, since the house was located much farther from the water than is mandated by codes, to save an ancient tree. Yet even among the plethora of similar sites in the San Juan Islands, this is a place of remarkable beauty, and the pavilion that is the major space of the house ideally captures that beauty, to which the saved ancient tree makes an extraordinary contribution (fig. 3.5). (The rock bench immediately outside the living space to the east was also a preexisting natural feature whose preservation was regarded as important, and the plan therefore carefully avoids it as well. Its proximity to the house, and its parallel relationship to the window wall, unfortunately carry the suggestion that the site was carved

**3.5** Retreat for Christian Grevstad and Terry Draheim, Decatur Island, WA, 1997–98: the view to the tree and the inlet, from the living pavilion. Suyama Architects.

to a flat plateau to accommodate the floor plane of the house. Suyama wishes it had been possible to bring a rock element into the house, to counter that suggestion.)

The budget was modest, and Suyama and Bruce Hinckley, who was a part of the design team from the outset, talked at length about what might be the simplest, most basic elements that would provide requisite shelter. A major volume was established by a simple, nearly square roof, resting on nine free-standing steel columns, with walls entirely of glass to offer the least possible separation from nature consistent with human occupancy (fig. 3.6). This volume is penetrated by three subordinate wood-walled volumes. The theme of a largely transparent pavilion partaking of the landscape, with subordinate, largely opaque volumes to accommodate activities demanding privacy or a sense of enclosure, would inform several of Suyama's subsequent

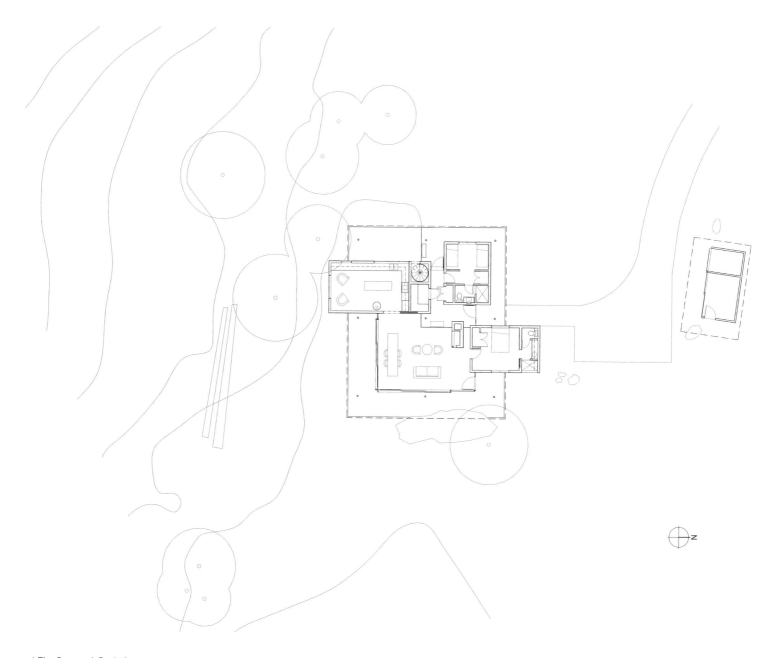

**3.6** The Grevstad-Draheim retreat: plan.

**3.7** The Grevstad-Draheim retreat: the approach from the north.

**3.8** The Grevstad-Draheim retreat: the entry; the bedroom volumes at left and right.

**3.9** The Grevstad-Draheim retreat: the living space, looking southeast.

projects. In those subsequent projects all of the largely opaque volumes would be lower than the transparent volume, but in the Grevstad design that is true only of the two that contain bedrooms; the kitchen and dining volume is much higher.

The Grevstad retreat is approached from the north (fig. 3.7) and is entered through the narrow throat between the two bedroom volumes (fig. 3.8). Beyond, an even narrower throat is created by the fireplace mass of concrete block, with steel hearth and mantle. The pavilion then opens to the south and the east, to prospects of the land, the ancient tree, and the sea (fig. 3.9). Since the columns of the pavilion's roof struc-

ture are independent of the walls, the glass wall panels can be slid aside, eliminating any architectural intervention whatsoever between the pavilion and the site. The bedrooms are the *yang* to the pavilion's *yin*; with their lower ceilings and largely opaque walls, they are small, snug sleeping refuges, appropriately withdrawn into the woods (fig. 3.10). The kitchen and dining areas are also given a more contained and introspective space for warmth and shelter on cold days, and in times of storm (fig. 3.11). Above the kitchen and dining volume, and the reason for its height, is a roof deck, which again looks to the remarkable view of the water seen through the branches of the ancient tree (fig. 3.12).

3.10 The Grevstad-Draheim retreat: the bedroom

3.11 The Grevstad-Draheim retreat: the kitchen.

3.12 The Grevstad-Draheim retreat: the deck above the kitchen, looking south.

**3.13** House for Gerald and Lynn Grinstein, Medina, WA, 1998–2001: the porte-cochere archway. Suyama Architects.

**3.14** The Grinstein house: the entry door

## THE LYN AND GERALD GRINSTEIN HOUSE

Lyn and Gerald Grinstein wanted a local architect for the new house they intended to build in Medina. After considering five and interviewing three, they chose George Suyama, perhaps partly because he shared Gerald Grinstein's passion for fly fishing, since what the Grinsteins had in mind was not at all typical of Suyama's work.

The Grinsteins had lived for many years in Fort Worth, in a magnificent neo-Elizabethan house of the 1920s—with walls of stone, half-timbering, arches and leaded windows, bays and balconies, beamed ceilings, a slate roof—designed for an earlier occupant by a distinguished architect from, surprisingly, Vancouver, British Columbia. In 1997, with many regrets about leaving the Texas house they had grown to love, they decided to return to their native Pacific Northwest. Having found a

waterfront lot in Medina, a Seattle suburb on the eastern shore of Lake Washington, they wanted to build something that would evoke the character of the Fort Worth house—something with stone walls (figs. 3.13, 3.14), a "library that looks like a library," a minstrel's gallery, robust timber trusses under a great pitched roof. The house was to be a setting, as well, for a significant art collection and for large-scale entertaining.

The house realizes the Grinsteins' intentions while also respecting Suyama's own way of designing; Hinckley speaks of Suyama's predilection for "modifying an old idea, pushing it to become something new." The entry hall does indeed include a "minstrel's gallery" (fig. 3.17), but that gallery is indebted as much to the catwalk-corridor of the Martin house project as to any Elizabethan interior. The robust timber trusses

**3.15** The Grinstein house: the entry door as seen from the hall, with full-height
bronze hinge.

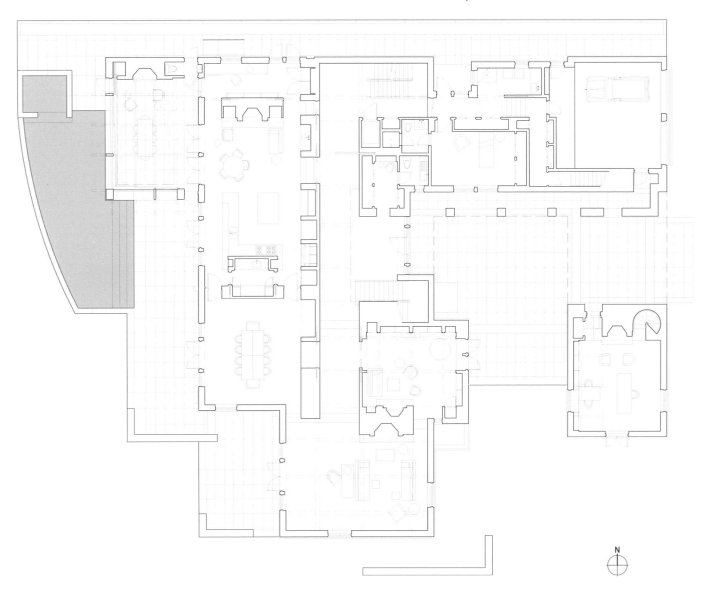

**3.16** The Grinstein house: plans

N

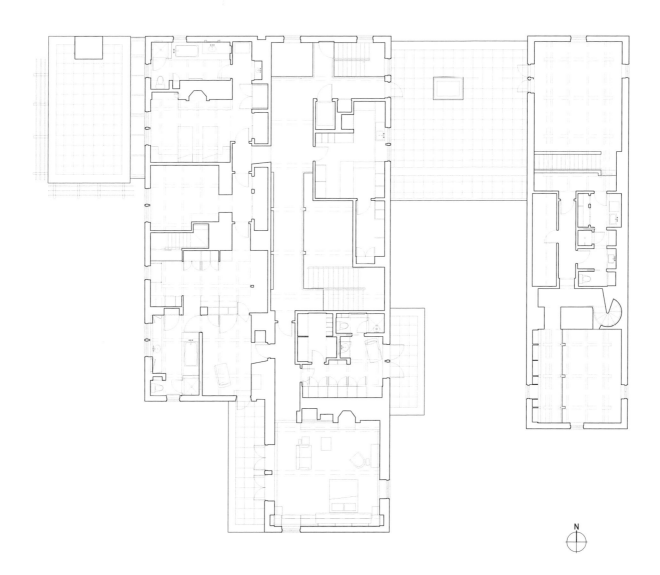

N

The Late Work

**3.17** The Grinstein house: the entry hall with "minstrel gallery."

**3.18** The Grinstein house: the family room.

support the roof for the entire length of the house and are exposed in most rooms. Granite was adopted for the walls throughout, and having accepted the choice of material, Suyama took the decision seriously: he determined the specific shapes of all key pieces of the granite walls— for some walls he drew the shape of every piece. (The material was from China, chosen for its quality and coloration. It was surprisingly inexpensive to obtain, even with shipping costs, but it proved to be very expensive to cut.) The segmentally arched ceilings in the family room,

dining room, and the eastern edge of the entry reinterpret Elizabethan examples while incorporating a lighting scheme that can be modified as needed. The panels are anchored with clips that tighten with vibration, hence they are proof against most earthquakes (fig. 3.18).

Floors are of white elm planks salvaged from nineteenth-century barns, with a radiant heating system underneath. The planks are much wider than usual, and though the installer could not guarantee that they would not warp, they have not. The wood is soft and subject to some

3.19 The Grinstein house: the library, looking east.

3.20 The Grinstein house: the library, looking west to the dining room.

marring, but the Grinsteins accept the patina; checks and splits, as they occasionally occur, are filled with epoxy.

The "library that looks like a library" (fig. 3.19) is one of Suyama's finest rooms. It is developed around a primary axis that is shared with the dining room across the corridor, and a secondary axis toward the living room's eastern edge. Within the room there is yet a third axis, that of the fireplace around which the furniture is grouped. The superb

detailing reminds us of Suyama's long experience with wood, while the ordered complexity of the composition again recalls the Martin project (fig. 3.20).

The westernmost element is the sun porch. All of its western glass panels slide north into a pocket, and all of the southern panels but one slide eastward, opening the corner of the room to the terrace and pool (fig. 3.21). The porch is completely separated from the house

3.21 The Grinstein house: the sun porch, looking southwest.

3.22 The Grinstein house: the sun porch, looking north toward the fireplace; the bath is at the juncture of sun porch and family room at right.

3.23 The Grinstein house: the sun porch: looking north, with glazed panels open.

by a glass zone that includes the door to the bath and the bath window (figs. 3.22, 3.23).

Even within the context of Suyama's work of this time, the Grinstein house of 1998–2001 is remarkable for its elegance of detail. Door hardware changes its metallurgy to accord with the mood of the space it faces (fig. 3.24). Pivoting doors that modify spaces retreat into niches to meld with hosting walls. Electrical amenities in baths and bedrooms are controlled by an array of white buttons within a stainless steel plate, flush with the cabinetwork, that is held in place magnetically—so much for high-tech. The basin in the powder room (fig. 3.25) needs only a bamboo dipper to complete the suggestion of a font at some ancient Shinto shrine.

3.24 The Grinstein house: door hardware.

3.25 The Grinstein house: the powder room.

Lyn Grinstein's terse evaluation: "It's a joy to live in a house of George's—every day I discover something new, every day a surprise."

THE FRANCES AND SCOTT MCADAMS RETREAT

The McAdams vacation retreat and Suyama's latest house for Kim and himself (deserving of a separate chapter) were in design and construction simultaneously, and they might be considered as urban and island versions of a shared theme. In each, a long, narrow volume is perpendicular, not parallel, to the shoreline; in each, a single simple roof, rectangular in plan, shelters and defines the primary volume.

In 1997 Frances and Scott McAdams bought a south-facing waterfront lot on San Juan Island, adjacent to the American Camp Park to the east and a neighborhood of undistinguished house types, not unlike mainland suburbia, to the west. The McAdams land slopes downward from the road at a significant gradient to become, eventually, an escarpment that drops away to a small and remarkably beautiful deeply recessed tidewater cove, framed by majestic boulder outcroppings to either side. The property included an existing house, unfinished, in poor condition, and "architecturally confused." Scott and Frances used the house for a few weekend getaways, but they knew at the time of purchase that they would demolish it and build anew. They wanted something small, in no way ostentatious, not "a typical suburban house"; they sought a retreat from their active Seattle city life, a place with no cable television, no Internet connection, no cell phone. They chose Suyama as their architect because, among several architects whose work they knew and liked, "George was the only one who seemed to grasp the idea of a simple life within a small dwelling."

In the spring of 1998, Suyama and Hinckley "showed up in a Land Rover and spent two hours crawling over every inch of the property, in the car, on foot, and on their hands and knees." They hiked the cove; the view from the eastern rock outcropping determined the arched form of the roof (fig. 3.26), as did the windswept dunes of American Camp Park; the house was to be a habitable "dune." Contemplating the developed land to the west, "Bruce pulled his coat over his head and said, 'I want to be shielded from the neighborhood by something like this'"; hence, the western concrete wall.

The basic concept evolved into a main volume opaque to the west and under an arching roof of north-south axis (fig. 3.27). The west edge of the roof rests on short columns that bear on the western wall; the eastern roof edge is borne on a range of columns lying slightly outboard of the eastern wall. The laminated wood beams that rest on these columns are exposed on the exterior, and on the interior they are clad by a ceiling of quarter-inch plywood panels (fig. 3.31) flexible enough to follow the curvature of the beams. Two long, opaque volumes that define the entry contain all storage, a washer and dryer, and the boiler for the radiant heating system in the concrete slab (fig. 3.29). The only other elements under the great roof are a bath at center, kitchen cabinetry

**3.26** The Scott and Frances McAdams retreat, San Juan Island, WA, 1998–2001: from the eastern rocks of the cove, looking north. Suyama Architects.

**3.27** The McAdams retreat: from the northwest.

**3.28** The McAdams retreat: the entry (center) from the motor court.

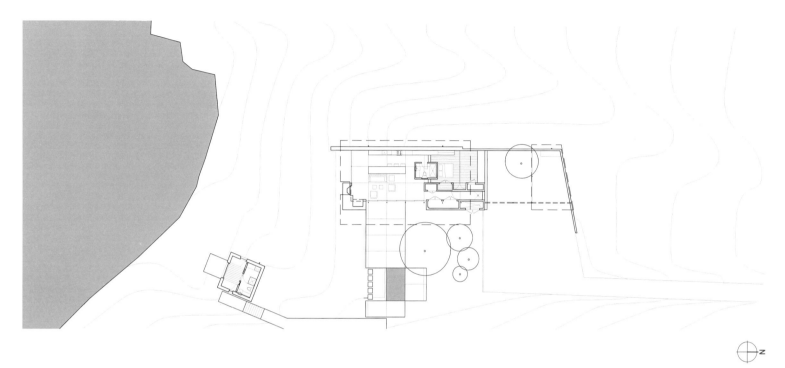

3.29 The McAdams retreat: plan.

3.30 The McAdams retreat: the entry.

along the western concrete wall, a concrete fireplace and woodbox mass at the southeast corner, and a great table, an integral part of the architecture, that runs the length of the living space.

Approaching the house from the north, one feels its recession into the earth; to enter one descends a few steps, walking between the two long walls (fig. 3.30). Immediately within, the walls continue, close to either side; only the fireplace mass is seen. Then, as one moves forward, the view opens to the falling land and the sea, toward which the house is felt to reach. A cross-axis is implied by the eastern wall of glazed sliding doors that open to the terrace and pool, but this axis is subordinate; the entry corridor, the bath, the kitchen, the great table, the cylinder of the roof overhead, all reinforce the seaward thrust (fig. 3.31). Even the

lateral terrace is directed seaward by the great windblown pine that emphatically closes the landward edge. The western concrete bastion ensures that other houses nearby are neither seen nor sensed. One is alone with the shelf of land that drops away to the sea.

Then, in the bedroom, all is reversed. A floor of ironwood, elevated by three steps, brings the ceiling closer, a desk and shelves comprise the north wall, the south wall is largely closet (fig. 3.33); there is no view whatsoever of the sea. The view through the glass wall to the north is of short reach and landward, into the little courtyard, with the gnarled trees beyond, seen against rising land (fig. 3.34).

The glazed bedroom wall does not include a door to the courtyard; Suyama admits that he wanted to keep the fenestration geometrically

**3.31** The McAdams retreat: the living space, looking south toward the cove and the sound. The table is a single plank of Douglas fir twenty feet in length, supported on steel piers.

**3.32** The McAdams retreat: the seaward steel pier of the table, with corner cutout for lamp cord, by craftsman David Gulassa.

pure. Most of the doors in the east wall of the bedroom serve a closet, but the one nearest the fenestration opens to a passage, short, narrow, and low, from which another door a few steps beyond opens into the little courtyard. The little secret passage seems to be enjoyed by all who traverse it, including Scott and Frances McAdams.

David Gulassa did many of the interior amenities, including both the wood and steel elements of the great table (fig. 3.32) and the steel elements of the sofa area. These were among his last works.

Eight years after its completion in 2001, the McAdamses still talk about the retreat as "a place of perfect peace."

The structure that was on the site at the time of their purchase was southeast of the new house and lay closer to the shoreline than present codes allow. Its preexistence made possible the little guest

**3.33** The McAdams retreat: the bedroom, looking southeast.

**3.34** The McAdams retreat: the bedroom, looking north.

*Overleaf:* **3.35** The McAdams retreat and the bunker exterior from the south.

house that also serves, now and then, as an alternate master bedroom. Puget Sound is ringed with the ruins of a network of naval gun emplacements that date from the late nineteenth and early twentieth centuries; the ruins are a dramatic part of the image of the region for those intimately familiar with it.[3] The guest house was intended to recall those ruins; hence, a pure cube of concrete, a bunker (fig. 3.35). Bruce Hinckley looks forward to its changing character over time: "It will get better and better as it weathers, slowly becoming clad with green moss and lichen." But unlike the ancient gun emplacements, the bunker is a geode. Its interior is an exquisite, tiny sleeping room and bath (fig. 3.36, 3.37), with floor of ironwood and walls of vertical-grain fir plywood, laser cut around the delicate wood frames of the small windows to east and west that bring light to the heads of the beds. Glass panels on the south

wall, between the beds, slide away to open the little space to the cove and the sea , in adventurous contrast to the land-oriented bedroom of the main house. For Frances and Scott, it is the sleeping place of choice in winter; within it, one confronts and defies the pelting gales that sweep northward from the sound into the strait.

### THE LAURIE AND GEORGE SCHUCHART HOUSE

Laurie and George Schuchart had lived for some years in Broadmoor, an old, established gated community near Lake Washington, well to the east of downtown Seattle. Unlike those of many similar, more recent communities, Broadmoor's lots are not particularly large, so its houses form a rather close-knit architectural fabric. The houses themselves date largely from the early decades of the twentieth century,

3.36 The McAdams retreat: the "bunker," the bedroom

3.37 The McAdams retreat: the "bunker," the bathroom

3.38 The McAdams retreat.

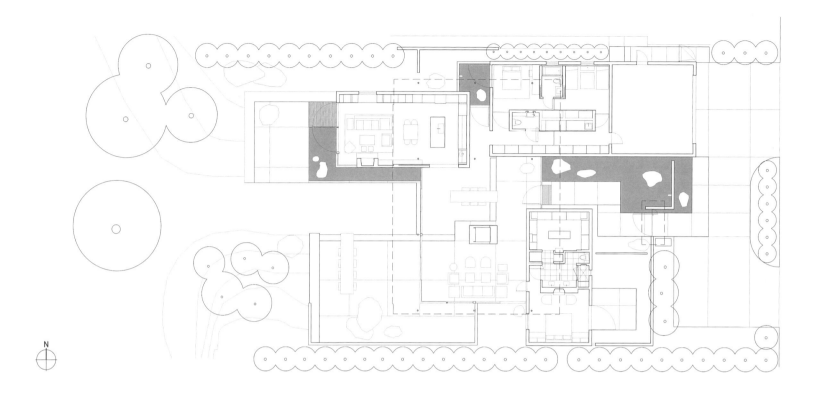

N

with several early modern examples from the 1950s; the Schucharts were living in a neo-medieval design from the 1920s. With the children grown, they were ready for a change, and in 2002 they bought a property a few lots south, intending to demolish the existing house thereon and build anew.

George Schuchart is a building contractor. In 1998 he submitted a bid to build the Grinstein house, and having done so was warned by fellow contractors that Suyama's way of designing was unusual and presented significant challenges for the builder. But the bid could hardly be withdrawn, and the Grinsteins chose Schuchart for the project. He found that the challenges were real enough, but he also found the process, and the product, surprisingly rewarding.

After interviewing three architects, the Schucharts decided on Suyama. Knowing Suyama's work as they did, the couple's original charge to him was brief and abstract: "light, organic materials, fire, and water."[4] Before any sketches were begun, indeed before they discussed the more pedestrian demands of the program, the Schucharts, Suyama, and Hinckley, who was by now almost Suyama's professional associate,

talked at length about the idea of camping, of being outdoors, gathered around the twilight fire. Their shared goal was to minimize, as far as possible, all differences between the interior and exterior spaces, extending the character of the architecture into the landscape and bringing the character of the landscape into the architecture. Although such an idea obviously poses real questions about how to provide for the practicalities of life—practicalities typically answered by bedrooms, baths, and kitchens—nevertheless, from the beginning, the idea of merging land and architecture was to underlie the design.

The existing house had rested on a low north-to-south ridge that rose about four feet above both Parkside Drive to the east and the golf course immediately to the west. Suyama and Hinckley both felt that the house should be "incised, tucked into the land."[5] They suggested that the ridge be leveled, to lower the profile of the new house toward the street and to bring its floor level to about the elevation of the golf course, thereby establishing a more intimate relationship with both the community and the land. (They had in mind a three-foot reduction in the height of the ridge, but the Schucharts felt that that would seem to be below the plane of the golf course, and excavation was stopped at two feet.) For similar reasons it was decided early on that the house should be on one floor, with modest changes in floor level to serve considerations of procession, scale, and outlook, and the boulders that are placed throughout the site should be included in the interiors as well, although they are fewer in number than Hinckley had originally intended.

Suyama conceived the spatial organization as "three boxes wrapped in glass," but that is not an entirely accurate description of the spatial concept. The plan is markedly similar to that of the Grevstad house and, as there, the "glass" that "wraps" the Schuchart "boxes" is in fact a grand glazed volume. Its high roof, a pure rectangle, is supported by three rows of three columns that lie either inside or outside, but never within, the walls of either the glazed volume or the boxes (fig. 3.39). Lateral rigidity is provided by the fireplace mass and by moment-resisting connections throughout the steelwork. Except where it is penetrated by the boxes, this high-glazed volume is everywhere entirely open to and closely integrated with the landscape, of which it is conceived as a part; from the beginning the space was to be "outside." Because of its integration with the landscape and its high ceiling, the glazed volume is felt to be the

dominant space, but the boxes comprise far and away the majority of the actual floor area. They, too, are simple rectangles in plan, with somewhat lower roofs and largely opaque walls. Far from being "wrapped," they lie about half under and half outside the high roof, penetrating the glazed volume only to a modest degree.

Off the sidewalk is a motor court, from which a pivoted gate—door, really—opens to a private courtyard (fig. 3.40). (The mandate for "organic materials" must have been quietly shelved at some point in the design process.) A walkway, with a pool on the right, doglegs to the entry to the house proper.

One enters on the plane of the entry walk (fig. 3.41), on a polished concrete floor that continues to the left into a sitting area; the fireplace/campfire rises from this floor plane. A lower floor lies ahead and at right in the dining area (fig. 3.42). This yields a still greater ceiling height for that area, but more importantly it creates a gentle declivity in both the architecture and the exterior elements beyond, tying the house more tightly to the land and thereby, paradoxically, bringing a strange intimacy to this otherwise grand space. Appropriately, the floor material in this area is wood. Both the lower and the upper areas open

**3.42** The Schuchart house: The dining area, and the lawn beyond, as seen from the entry.

**3.43** The Schuchart house: the sitting area as seen from the dining area, looking south.

**3.44** The Schuchart house: the sitting area, looking west.

to the landscape by means of glass panels that slide away like transparent un-mullioned shoji screens (figs. 3.43 and 3.44). The wood-floored lower level opens to lawn; the polished concrete upper floor opens to a polished concrete terrace.

The "box" to the west comprises the kitchen, dining, and a much-used alternate living space, whose thick north wall provides storage and a small working desk (fig. 3.46). Two pivoting glazed panels open the room to the garden and to a wooden deck that crosses the pool to become a dining terrace (figs. 3.47 and 3.48). The master bedroom is reached by a door from the upper conversation area of the glazed vol-

ume (fig. 3.49), and here the contrast in spatial experience from pavilion to box is felt most strongly; the lower ceiling and the opaque walls create a snug sleeping refuge. A pivoting glazed panel opens the room to its own intimate courtyard (fig. 3.50). The western guest bedroom opens to its little pool-strewn rockery (fig. 3.51). The eastern guest bedroom has no similar garden outlook; a special illumination compensates. All of the boxes are clad in the horizontal wood siding that has become Suyama's typical material for this purpose. It is custom milled, and its vertical dimension is a module that governs all other vertical dimensions throughout the house.

**3.45** The Schuchart house: the dining space, looking toward the kitchen and family room.

**3.46** The Schuchart house: the kitchen and family room, looking east. The entry to the house is visible at right; the cantilevered bookshelves are at far right.

**3.47** The Schuchart house: the kitchen and family room, looking west; the desk at right, and ahead the pivoting glazed panels that can open to the terrace beyond.

**3.48** The Schuchart house: the family room terrace and pool, looking east, with the glazed wall panels swung open.

**3.49** The Schuchart house: the sitting area looking southeast, with the entry to the master bedroom at center.

**3.50** The Schuchart house: the master bedroom, looking east, with the pivoting panel opened to the small courtyard.

**3.51** The Schuchart house: the view from the western guest bedroom to its micro-garden.

**3.52** The Schuchart house: the western guest bedroom, looking south toward the hall.

3.53 The Schuchart house: the master bath shower; the window to the small courtyard, with "shutters" open.

3.54 The Schuchart house: the master bath shower, with "shutters" half closed.

The distinguishing strengths of the Schuchart design lie in its oneness with its site, and the extraordinary creativeness and craft of its details, for which the master bath and dressing room, the guest powder room, and the family room bookshelves may serve as examples.

A window in the master bath shower looks out on the master bedroom's small courtyard. Laurie felt that this window compromised privacy, since the courtyard wall is only eight feet high and does not block sight lines from Broadmoor's tree-trimmers. With some reluctance Suyama endorsed the point and designed the eight-inch-deep jambs of the sixteen-inch-wide window as bronze shutters (figs. 3.53

and 3.54). Closet doors typically lie within a quarter of an inch of the ceiling and floor (figs. 3.52, 3.55), which means that, if the doors are to swing freely, both ceiling and floor must be absolutely planar. This in turn obviates the usual gypsum plasterboard for the ceiling, since its slightly bulging taped joints make a truly planar surface impossible. The ceilings, then, must be of plaster, applied to an astonishing standard, and the floors must be of meticulously laid flooring. A similar exactness is necessary at the threshold of the door from the pavilion to the master bedroom: the surface of the pavilion's polished concrete floor, and that of the bedroom's carpet, are exactly co-planar, demanding, again,

**3.55** The Schuchart house: the master dressing room.

an extraordinary precision in the pouring of both concrete slabs. The horizontal boards that clad typical opaque walls are a custom-milled size and profile. The first run delivered to the site was off in width by 1/16 of an inch. Because the error would, in the height of any given wall, be cumulative, the entire order had to be re-run to exact dimension. Similar conditions apply throughout the house, for similar reasons.

The powder room along the storage corridor of the guest bedroom unit includes a stainless steel basin with storage below. The top quarter-inch of the basin continues around the room as a narrow stainless steel trim strip (fig. 3.56). It is echoed in vertical trim strips at the midpoints of all four walls. Around these the plaster must again be applied to an astonishing standard of craftsmanship, since in all cases it stops a fraction of an inch outside the stainless strip—the architectural term for this gap is "reveal" or "quirk." The vertical stainless strips continue onto the ceiling, to terminate in the round skylight (fig. 3.57).

Finally, the bookshelves in the family room are steel plates cantilevering from the wall (see fig. 3.46) and anchored to the wall studs before the plaster wall surface is applied. The plaster is then applied around them, with, as elsewhere, a quirk of a fraction of an inch between plaster and steel.

George Schuchart says of the house: "I work all week, the weekend comes, I wonder why we don't go away somewhere—but I'm so happy just being here, I love being here. The land and the building are one."[6] But he notes, too, that constructing this architecture is "slow and careful work, hard to schedule, hard to budget." The little powder room in itself took three months to build: "The entire box is conceptually a piece of cabinetwork." This way of designing and building is costly, but its objective is not ostentation, rather it is the satisfaction that devolves from meticulous craftsmanship. To find an architecture of equal perfection, it may well be that one must go back to the buildings of Ise, or those on the Athenian Acropolis.

The Schuchart house received the only 2005 AIA Honor Award for Seattle. The jury said of it: "We found everything to admire in this design, most specifically the integration of the interior and exterior spaces, the placement of the house in the landscape, and the selection and detailing of materials. Each exterior space relates directly to a dedicated private exterior space, while the house and gardens benefit from and add to the wider landscape beyond the site." Significantly, the jury's comments speak to the close collaboration among Suyama, Schuchart, and Hinckley. George Schuchart remembers his surprise at the degree to which "George [Suyama] listened to and even deferred to us, and especially to Bruce."

1. From the David Gulassa Web site; Suyama's comments at the time of Gulassa's death.
2. George Suyama, "Preface," in *Wind: A Sound Translation by Patrick Zentz*, the brochure for the installation of May 7–July 22, 1999.
3. These include Fort Casey at the eastern tip of Whidbey Island, Fort Flagler and Fort Worden opposite Fort Casey across Admiralty Inlet near Port Townsend, and Fort Ward on the southwest shore of Bainbridge Island. All, in their day, included the conventional military buildings, and a separate elaborate concrete warren to serve a "disappearing" gun battery, the guns retracting below a concrete parapet, for concealment and protection when not in use. Though the guns themselves were naval ordnance, the posts were under the command of the army. The guns from all four sites were removed in World War II for other uses; a single example has been replaced at both Fort Casey and Fort Worden. At Forts Casey, Worden, and Flagler, both the support buildings and the concrete warren still exist; at Fort Ward, the support buildings are gone. The concrete ruins suggest, at a smaller scale, the emplacements of the German Atlantic Wall of World War II.
4. Laurie Schuchart interview, 15 November 2007.
5. Bruce Hinckley interview, 7 December 2007.
6. George Schuchart interview, April 3, 2009.

**3.56** The Schuchart house: the guest powder room; the basin.

3.57 The Schuchart house: the guest powder room; the skylight.

# 4

The clients had thought, at first, of remodeling the house in which they were living, on the northernmost lot of the eventual site. But they had acquired a major art collection that includes many large-scale pieces, and the gallery they wished to build for its display would be, of necessity, far too large for the existing property. They were able to buy the three contiguous lots to the south, and, one thing leading to another, they decided to build, as a single project, both a gallery and a new home.

They wanted a Northwest architect. They interviewed several and chose George Suyama because of what they believed to be his unique grasp of gallery lighting and his long-standing involvement with the arts community. Design began early in 1997, construction in September of 1998, with a good bit of the design evolving in the course of construction. The project was completed in September of 2002. Ric Peterson was project manager; Jay Deguchi, who in the course of the project would become the firm's third partner, was lead designer.

The site is in Medina, on the eastern shore of Lake Washington (fig. 4.1). From the shore, the land rises steeply to a relatively level plateau, about forty feet above lake level, that in earlier decades had hosted an apple orchard; hence the project's name. The southern third of the site is claimed by a preexisting house, the new garage, and a range of trees and low walls screening a sculpture court; a parking court is at the northern edge. A funicular at the northwestern corner of the plateau provides access to the lake shore.

The new house and gallery are composed roughly in the shape of a broad U with unequal legs (figs. 4.1, 4.2, 4.3). The house, which comprises the northwestern part of the complex, is unlike Suyama's typical contemporaneous residential compositions in that two floors of residential spaces are grouped under two sloped roofs, separated at the apex by a clerestory. The lower roof, nearest the lake, shelters formal living and dining rooms and a family living room, and, in a northeastward extension, a breakfast room. Under the higher roof are, on the lower floor, a glass gallery, a library/media room, and a kitchen; and on the upper floor, master and guest bedrooms and the client's study and workspace. The southern part of the lower roof, ascending toward the east, shelters the major gallery space. South of the gallery, under lower flat roofs, are rooms ancillary to the gallery, and a swimming pool

**4.1** The Orchard, Medina, Washington, 1997–2002: the model of house and gallery as they might be seen in aerial view from the northwest. Suyama Architects/Suyama Peterson Deguchi.

**4.2** The Orchard; the house and gallery as seen in aerial view from the southeast.

(fig. 4.4). A lengthy entry drive meanders through a landscape shared by the remaining trees of the orchard and several outdoor sculpture pieces from the clients' collection.

For what is ostensibly a residence, this is a very large building indeed, yet its great size, which might have been overwhelming, is nowhere evident from the ground plane. The building is screened from houses to the south by continuous tall plantings, and lying to the north of them as it does, it blocks none of their sunlight. Within the site itself, the entry court is framed by a composition of walls the most dominant of which, at left of the entry path (fig. 4.5), is not itself overwhelming in dimension, but its height and location block any view of the great volume that is the gallery wing. This wall, opening at its midpoint to a view of an obelisk, introduces the ashlar masonry vocabulary of minute horizontal strata that will occur throughout the residential spaces.

One enters by turning left at the end of this wall (fig. 4.6), then turning right, toward the lake; the entry door was fabricated by Boater's Blacksmith. The corridor that lies ahead (fig. 4.7) marks the seam between gallery and residence.

Immediately left is what is called the entry gallery (fig. 4.8). To the west and south, the floor plane is recessed and is of black basalt; the effect is of a moat, and it is appropriately skylit. From this space one moves eastward along a gentle ramp onto an intermediate plateau, from which three steps lead down into the gallery proper (fig. 4.9).

The gallery was studied in computer simulations to examine structural possibilities, but the design of the space itself was developed by means of several large-scale wooden study models, one of them four feet in length with removable roof and walls. Photocopies of all major paintings and photography and three-dimensional approximations of

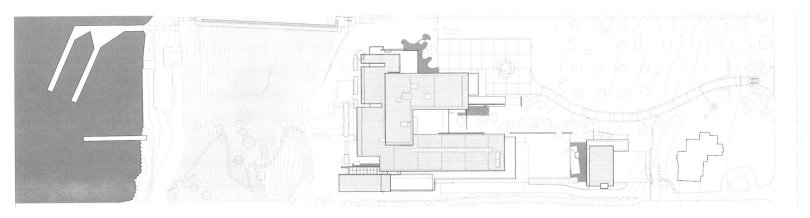

**4.3** The Orchard: plans, site plan.

N

The Orchard

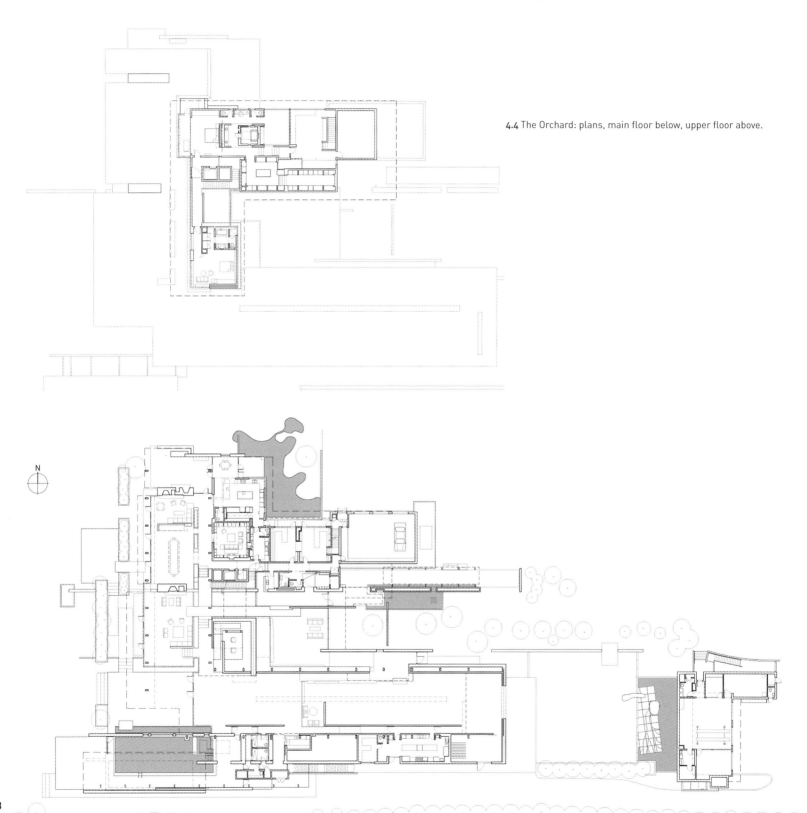

4.4 The Orchard: plans, main floor below, upper floor above.

**4.6** The Orchard: the entry walk near the entry, looking south toward the gallery. The wall's masonry is typical of that throughout the residence.

**4.7** The Orchard: the entry hall looking west toward the lake, with the entry gallery ahead at left.

all sculptural work were made to scale and fitted to these models to ensure adequate wall area and spatial provision, and to test the relationships between the pieces within the space. (Jay Deguchi acknowledges the influence of Carlo Scarpa in the design, and especially Scarpa's Castelvecchio Museum in Verona of 1958–64.)

The gallery is patently a single volume, and its dimensions are those of a major public space; this can be seen most dramatically in figure 4.2, in which the gallery is seen in the context of neighboring houses, themselves quite large. Yet this great volume is, on the interior, remarkably unintimidating. This may be true, in part, because it *is* a gallery; interesting things are everywhere, and many of them are of no remarkably great size. But this is the case with the architecture, too: the space is shaped by an extraordinary number of autonomous floor, wall, and ceiling surfaces, none of which extends to any full dimension of the space. These surfaces, furthermore, are complex in their junctures, or rather their absence of junctures: they float, they shift, they are cloven for windows and skylights, they slide by one another like Suyama's sliding and pivoting walls; there is no fully closed corner in the entire vast

**4.8** The Orchard: the entry gallery looking north.

4.9 The Orchard: the main gallery, looking east.

4.10 The Orchard: the living room and and the west end of the main gallery seen from the residential corridor, looking south. The windows open to a view of Lake Washington and Seattle.

volume. Thus the volume seems to have been created by means of an assemblage of elements none of which is of the scale of the space itself. In the western third of the space, as the ceiling descends, the floor plane is elevated by two risers, giving that part of the space a significantly reduced vertical dimension. The western wall of windows (fig. 4.10), opening to a terrace and a view of Lake Washington and Seattle, twists, at its northern extremity, through five corners as it wraps itself around a narrow black basalt moat to become the southern wall of the formal reception room (fig. 4.11). Here, too, the corners are not solids but voids, not mullions but butted glass.

Although the gallery is flooded with natural light, the relationship of the light to the art material is meticulously controlled. The skylight that runs through much of the length of the ceiling, on its approximate centerline, is designed to admit only northern light. The windows at the northeast corner admit northern light and a modicum of morning sun; a skylight above the upper southern portion of that eastern wall washes the wall with light, which, in turn, is reflected into the space as ambient light. The broad skylight at the southwest corner of the gallery is designed so that it admits direct sunlight, but not onto any display surface.

**4.11** The Orchard: the western end of the gallery, looking northwest. The formal living room is at center.

**4.12** The Orchard: the family room fireplace wall.

This is an extraordinary room. It is a space of remarkable and pervasive complexity, yet among those who experience it, the most commonly expressed reaction is a sense of palpable serenity.

The formal living room is northwest of the main gallery (fig. 4.11). It has in common with the residential spaces generally that the materials of its surfaces are darker in value and coloration, and are composed of more finely scaled elements, than the galleries. Directly north is the formal dining room, intended to accommodate large groups, and beyond, the family room for the owners' private hours. East are the kitchen and breakfast room, opening to a small courtyard, designed by landscape architect Rich Haag, that emulates a traditional Japanese garden, complete with koi pool. The average ceiling height in the formal living room is twelve feet; the elevated floor plane in the dining and family rooms brings the ceiling in those spaces to a somewhat more intimate ten-foot height, and the lower roof plane over the kitchen and breakfast space yields a nine-foot ceiling.

The mechanical and electrical systems for the house, gallery, and pool occupy a basement space many times the size of an average house. Apart from the normal demands of a residence of such vast extent, these systems include fire-alarms and sprinklers, elaborate security provi-

4.13 The Orchard: the stair to the upper floor.

4.14 The Orchard: the swimming pool.

sions, and equipment to control temperature and humidity with extraordinary precision and reliability. Both clients and architect intended that all aspects of these extensive utilities installations should reflect the design quality of the building as a whole. Yet designing every conduit and duct, every water line, filter, heater, and condenser, every control panel and valve, and ensuring, through supervision, their installation as designed, is well outside the abilities of any architectural office. Of necessity such matters must fall to the respective subcontractors. The subcontractors, therefore, were challenged to make their provisions works of art, and to submit detailed descriptions—shop drawings—of their installations toward that end. The success of this team process is astonishing (fig. 4.15).*

* Some comparable examples may exist, but the only one I am aware of that can stand shoulder to shoulder with this space is the mechanical room of the Edsel Ford Estate in Grosse Pointe, Michigan, of 1927–28, by Albert Kahn.

# Fauntleroy II

*water running through*
*rooms of quieting delight*
*sand and sound below*
—Richard Smith

The Vashon Island ferry has come and gone dozens of times a day for at least half a century, from a shallow cove in the shoreline of the West Seattle neighborhood known as Fauntleroy. Yet along the shores north and south of the ferry dock there is still a salt sea smell. Shellfish are in the sand and the tidepools and on the rocks; kelp and driftwood mark the high line of recent tides. Vashon and Bainbridge Islands, not so far away to the west across the sound, are visible in almost any weather. On a clear day Bremerton can be seen beyond Bainbridge, against the background of the Olympic mountain range on the horizon.

Kim and George Suyama had moved into their house in the cove, on a site north of the dock, in 1987. Shortly thereafter, they attended a neighborhood party on the beach, a hundred yards south of the dock. The lot on which the party occurred is, in its dimensions and topography, typical of those around it, and is not unlike the site on which

the Suyamas were then living. West-facing and 50 feet wide by 200 feet deep, it slopes modestly upward from the water, then rises sharply to a higher plateau that then ascends quite gently toward the sidewalk and the street. The lot is atypical, however, in that, near the shore, within a grove of four ancient firs, two fishermen's shelters remained from some indefinite time in the early decades of the twentieth century (fig. 5.1). Kim and George decided at once that if the lot were ever for sale, they would buy it. In 1997 it was, and they did.

The southern of the two fishermen's shelters is a tiny single room, which the Suyamas used at first only for storage. Now fitted with fishing gear, a mounted fish high on the south wall, a bed with comforter, and a washbasin, it can accommodate a single guest in marine romanticism. The other shelter the Suyamas renovated to serve as their home; it would do so for four years. It sits on higher land than its southern compatriot, and its 550 square feet include a living space, a bedroom, a bath, and a kitchen and dining space. The entry is midway along the southern façade, although here "façade" seems not the right word (fig. 5.2). The tiny living room, a snug haven with a useful working fireplace on the northern wall (fig. 5.3), looks out to Puget Sound from an elevation

5.1 The second house on the Fauntleroy cove for George and Kim Suyama ("Fauntleroy II"), 1998–2001: from the sound. The smaller fisherman's cottage is at right, the larger at left. Suyama Architects.

that, in a storm, seems barely above the waves. The bedroom amidships accommodates a double bed with no space to spare. The landward kitchen and dining space are commensurately diminutive. Inevitably Kim and George felt the limitations of the little cottage at times, but they cherished their time there, and they cherish the little house still. It now serves as a guest cottage and, occasionally, as an alternate master bedroom.

The house on the plateau above, built in the 1940s, was unlike the northern cottage in being of conventional size, and unlike it too in being of no distinction whatever. From the beginning the Suyamas meant to replace it. "The only part of the site that felt good was the cabin area—we loved the cabins. But I knew George could fix the house. I didn't worry about a thing." In 1998 George, with Bruce Hinckley and associates Peterson and Deguchi, began the design. The process would encompass three years, and would evolve through at least seven schemes, largely because of the Suyamas' changing view of the kind of life they sought to lead. Their earlier Fauntleroy house had been densely furnished; George had indulged his urge to acquire antiques, and Kim had the piano and her own numerous acquisitions. The move to the little cottage had forced a paring down to essential possessions, and thereby a rethinking of a way of life. Of necessity Kim and George sold almost all of their collection of accoutrements, and found themselves liberated thereby. George says the experience led him to see architecture as "a tool that might allow one to live in a different and better way, might offer a freedom to get rid of paraphernalia." Each successive scheme for the new house, therefore, was smaller than its predecessor.

A criterion from the outset was that the new house must not intimidate the cottage. Since the cottage lies in the northern third of the site, that third, therefore, must have only subordinate architectural elements, and so far as possible they must be withdrawn eastward from the escarpment. The main body of the house, then, must lie within the southern 30 feet or so of the lot, from which a requisite 8-foot side-yard setback on the south would leave available something like a 22-foot width; hence the house must essentially lie within a long east-west rectangle. In the final scheme, elements within that boundary include a garage, a powder room and closet, and two very different living spaces on two floors. All lie under the shelter of a simple rectangular roof, slightly sloped from north to south, that, including its generous overhangs, is 27 feet wide and fully 120 feet long (fig. 5.4). On the north side of these elements, and penetrating them slightly, is an almost autonomous volume a half-level down from the main floor. The zone of penetration is claimed by the stair that accesses the bedroom

**5.2** Fauntleroy II: The larger cottage, the front entry

**5.3** Fauntleroy II: The larger cottage, the living room

**5.4** Fauntleroy II: the site plan.

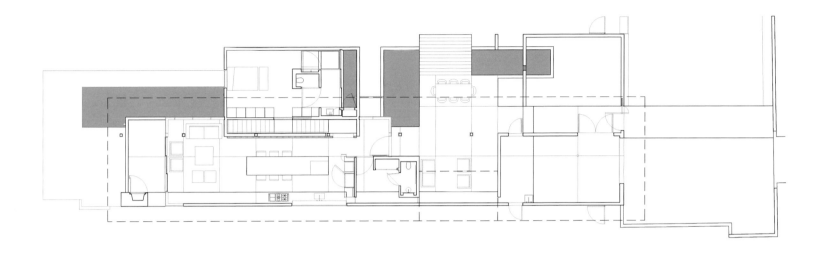

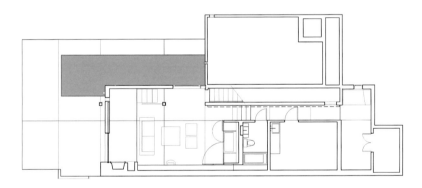

**5.5** Fauntleroy II: upper and lower floor plans.

**5.6** Fauntleroy II: as seen from the street to the east.

**5.7** Fauntleroy II: in the motor court, with the pivoting gate (door?) to the first courtyard under the roof edge at left.

**5.8** Fauntleroy II: in the first courtyard, looking west, with the entry to the second courtyard at left and the beginning of the watercourse at extreme right.

in the mid-level volume, then continues down to the lower living space (fig. 5.5). The northern third of the site also includes an all-important watercourse in various manifestations.

One enters from the street through a broad opening in the wall that lies just inboard of the sidewalk (fig. 5.6); a simple courtyard is at right. Ahead, under the right edge of the roof (fig. 5.7), a pivoting panel opens to a second courtyard within which is a pool, whose water flows in a channel through a low opening in the courtyard's western wall (fig. 5.8). Beyond this wall, the concrete floor extends north to the edge of a second pool that is fed by the channel from the preceding courtyard; a floor of wood slats reaches across about half of this pool (fig. 5.9). At left is a space that, in all respects except the absence of a fourth wall, is a living room (fig. 5.10). This space has some precedent in the courtyards of the Lumpkin and Campbell houses and the earlier Fauntleroy house, and those, in turn, may be indebted to Zema's Whidbey Island composition. But this space is far different from any of its predecessors: with its

**5.9** Fauntleroy II: the second courtyard, looking southwest; the entry to the house proper is at center.

**5.10** Fauntleroy II: the second courtyard; the outdoor room.

5.11 Fauntleroy II: from the second courtyard, the entry to the house at center.

5.12 Fauntleroy II: the interior; the kitchen, dining, and living spaces, looking west.

cabinetwork, fireplace, seating, and, above all, its roof, it is much more explicitly an indoor room minus a wall. George finds some emotional comfort in the evident possibility of movement, even escape—perhaps a vestige of his earliest years in the internment camps—and it may be that this room without a wall is for him a source of that emotional comfort.

Ahead is the entry to the interior (fig. 5.11). At right a glass wall reveals the watercourse as now a narrow steel aqueduct above a chasm. At left a windowless volume provides a generous space for removing coats, a closet, and a powder room. Beyond is a single space that includes what, in a typical residential plan, would be kitchen, dining, and living spaces. At its distant end it opens to a deck and to the sound (fig. 5.12). But the view to the sound is only slowly revealed, through a seemingly orchestrated processional experience.

As with the McAdams retreat on San Juan Island, all elements of the space—the window and counter at left, the great table, and the long low wall at right—lead the eye seaward. The window and the cabinets and counter on the south wall are the most forceful of these elements, and they are detailed with an extraordinary finesse. The thirty-inch-high cabinets are open-front boxes of blued plate steel, fabricated by Tod von Mertens, supported by steel fins that rest on the polished concrete floor;

the cabinet doors are of lacquered, high-density particle board that can easily be mistaken for blued steel. The counter in a kitchen space, however, is typically at a thirty-six-inch height, and resolving the disparity between this and the thirty-inch cabinet height typical elsewhere is a classic architectural problem. The solution here is elegantly minimalist: in the kitchen zone the thirty-inch steel cabinets are surmounted by a six-inch, black granite slab into which the sink and range are recessed (fig. 5.13). Above the granite, the long horizontal window is set within a deep steel frame, which, extended to the right in an early remod-

eling, frames an upward-pivoting range hood, then a spice cabinet. Opposite the sink and range is a steel construction, also fabricated by von Mertens, that serves as kitchen counter, and serves, too, to anchor the eastern end of the eighteen-foot-long table, cut from a twenty-six-foot slab of Douglas fir, that dominates the space. The space is edged to the north by the low opaque wall with clerestory above and beyond. Westward, beyond this wall, the space widens to the plane of the clerestory to become a sitting space, small in plan but expanded by the tremendous view that opens—to the sound and the distant horizon to the

5.13 Fauntleroy II: the main interior looking east.

5.14 Fauntleroy II: the sitting space looking west, with the deck beyond.

west, and the ferry dock and the near vegetation to the north (fig. 5.14). Beyond is the deck, for which the steel-cabinet volume becomes the firewood box and the outdoor fireplace (fig. 5.15). From the deck's edge, the shore and the two little fishermen's dwellings can be seen.

Since the house was necessarily close to the southern lot line, for reasons of privacy the south wall had to be largely opaque; not much direct southern sun enters the house. Most designers in the Puget Sound region adopt the conventional wisdom of opening the southern side of a house in every possible way, to garner a maximum of

**5.15** Fauntleroy II: the deck, looking north.

**5.16** Fauntleroy II: the shaded sitting space, and sunlit vegetation.

direct sunlight in a region that is not known for its profusion. Suyama's approach, however, although here driven by other considerations, is common in Japan, and it offers alternative advantages. With the more typical southern orientation, one looks from a brightly lit space to shaded material beyond. With a northern orientation, as here, one looks from a softly lit space toward sunlit material, in this case vegetation and the watercourse (fig. 5.16). And in late summer afternoons, the sun in the southwest penetrates both living spaces and casts a golden light on the landscape elements; George especially enjoys those times as contrast to the midday experience.

The low wall that slightly pinches the middle zone of the living space is, conceptually, the southern face of the prism that is slid into the major volume a half-level below the living space. In the interstitial space so created, a stair descends that half level to the bedroom and bath for which the inserted prism exists, the stair belonging, as it were, to both the major volume and the inserted prism. The bedroom is carefully

5.17 Fauntleroy II: the bedroom, looking west.

5.18 Fauntleroy II: the bedroom looking east toward the bath and the waterfall wall.

5.19 Fauntleroy II: the lower living space in two levels, with the glass pocket door to access the shower at left.

composed as an elemental Euclidean space, and unlike the main floor that leads, eventually, to a sweeping view, this space is introverted, lit by a single square window centered in the western wall (fig. 5.17). Suyama speaks of reducing visual noise; there is no better example in his work than this room, whose hard-won visual simplicity yields a haven of utter repose.

The bath, however, although it also seems elemental on plan, is spatially complex. Only the toilet space is bounded by fixed walls, and it has no conventional door. A pivoting panel can close it, and in doing so allow views from the bedroom to a light well—the eastern boundary of the bath—into which the watercourse falls from the aqueduct that was seen from the entry above (fig. 5.18). Alternatively, the panel can pivot to close the basin area and the toilet room from the bedroom. A similar panel north of the toilet room, when turned to close the view from the bedroom to the light well, reveals the shower facilities and creates the shower stall.

Another half-flight of the stair leads down to what is misleadingly called, on plan, basement storage; it is in, fact, another living space on two levels, the upper of which, reached by a short steel stair, provides the major access from the house to the shore (fig. 5.20). Along the north edge of this space the watercourse ends as a pool, to which a great pivoting window opens. A long corridor adjacent to the stair leads eastward and upward to a guest room and a wine cellar.

All seems composed, all seems resolved. Yet this is an architecture as rich in ambiguities and multivalences as anything proposed by post-modernism or deconstructionism. Is the entry to the second courtyard the entry to the house, or is it a garden gate? If it is the entry to the house, as its decisively architectural character might lead one to think, what, then, is the next "entry"? What of the space under the great roof, with fireplace and three walls but not four: is it a room, or a terrace, or a garden folly? Do we consider it an exterior space, or is it interior? Does it in fact have a fourth wall in the northern vegetation? The cabinets in the major interior space that, at their eastern end, belong to the kitchen, become several different things on their long journey to the western

edge of the deck, as does the kitchen window on its shorter westward journey. What do we call the table? Is it a dining table? Yes—and no. Does the stair belong to the major volume under the simple rectangular roof, or is it part of the inserted bedroom box? What of the wall that is the stair's southern edge? And how do we assign, or define, or even describe, the panels in the master bath, late progeny of those in the Benaroya condominium, that modify both the bedroom and the bath spaces? When are the panels "open"? When "closed"? Do "open" and "closed" have any unambiguous meaning here?

Yet these ambiguities and multivalences do not derive from the appropriation of movements in literary criticism, nor are they meant as commentary, either witty or profound, on social, political, or moral positions. They are architectural in their essence; they derive from

5.20 Fauntleroy II: the lower living space; the stair connecting the two levels.

5.21 Fauntleroy II: the upper living space, looking south.

considerations of space and use and materials and site; they derive from the creating of open and contained, light and dark, up and down. And they serve an ambience, not of witticism or conflict or confusion, but of resolution and tranquility.

The house was the recipient of an AIA Honor Award for Washington Architecture. The jury noted:

The Fauntleroy Residence stands out as an instance of masterful design, an achievement of international stature. Informed by a worldly understanding of architectural possibility, the residence nevertheless engages its context and site at every level. Seattle's climate—mild, sometimes wet, sometimes dry—is welcomed with deep overhanging eaves and the patient sequencing of rooms alternately open and enclosed, covered and uncovered. The site's history is evident in two original structures, small beachside cabins, and the use of the prior residence's foundation and porch as a transition between the new structure and the old. At the most basic level, the design emphasizes the long, narrow lot itself. A continuous stream engages the house along its northern edge, narrowing and then pooling in the way that people, moving through the house, flow or pause and then gather. Alongside it, the program unfolds in a syncopated series of spaces that step easily from the modest streetfront into shelter, then enclosure, and open finally onto views of water and mountains framed by the two cabins and a tall cluster of one-hundred-year-old Douglas firs.

This house exhibits tremendous sureness of hand, never needing to stray from its essential conceptual ideas to generate the logic of its details. At ease with its transitions and variety, simple and exacting in both materials and craft, the Fauntleroy residence is a deeply personal, world-class achievement.

# 6

In the first two years of life, even though one retains no
explicit memories (Freud called this infantile amnesia),
deep emotional memories or associations are nevertheless being made in the limbic system and other
regions of the brain where emotions are represented—
and these emotional memories may determine one's
behavior for a lifetime.

—Oliver Sacks

George had intended that the second Fauntleroy house "offer a freedom to get rid of paraphernalia," but he and Kim are both aware that it
does so only in a relative sense. Its architecture, including the extensive
watercourse, is only in a limited way a manifestation of a simpler life.

The Suyamas own the vacant lot immediately to the north. It is
of the same dimensions as that of the existing house: 50 feet wide, 200
feet deep, sloping some 26 feet, at mean tide, from sidewalk to shore.
The topography, however, is quite different. Immediately west of the
sidewalk the contours drop away quite sharply into a natural bowl that
becomes a pronounced swale continuing westward to the shore; this
swale was in earlier times a stream bed. The only evidences of the hand
of man on the site are a small cabin and the remains of a rhododendron
garden. For some time Kim and George have talked of selling the existing house, and building, on the north lot, something that would realize
a different ambition. Of that ambition, George says

> The architect today is forced to build objects that satisfy
> an elaborate range of "needs." I would like to do the exact
> opposite—I'd like to create a pure shelter that accommo-
> dates nothing we are forced to deal with today. Kim and I
> go back and forth—she asks what I will do with all the art;
> I'm interested in art as nature, the trees as walls. What is
> wrong with what I have been doing is that I haven't had this
> sense of what is important to me.

George's words imply an elemental, diminutive architecture, minimal and spare, within a setting of indigenous wild grasses and vines
that will merge with the driftwood, the kelp and shellfish, on the salt-
sea shore. There are in the concept resonances of the Primitive Hut of
Vitruvius and Laugier, the primordial prototype of architecture. In this

**6.1** The third house on the Fauntleroy cove for George and Kim Suyama ("Fauntleroy III"), 1998–2001: the model, view from the northeast. Suyama Peterson Deguchi.

vision we come full circle architecturally. We also come full circle in George's life, for he is inclined to think that his longing for the minimal, the primal, may be a remnant of his years of infancy in the Minidoka camp, that he retains a deep association with what must have been the desperately intense affections among family and friends at that time, in that place.

Yet George is aware, too, that he may carry other emotions from Minidoka, that he is equally driven by a revulsion for that environment,

a deep rejection of that grim austerity. And there are other considerations. Kim gave up the piano with the move to the waterfront cottage, and the existing house has no place for it. She would like to play again, would like to return the making of music to her everyday life. George has given much to the visual arts, and the examples he possesses, few but deliberately chosen, are dear to him. They require surfaces on which to occur. Both George and Kim derive pleasure from evenings with friends, and evenings with friends entail a generous hospitality, which in turn

demands a spatial adequacy. And many of the Suyamas' furnishings have been done by artisans who are, or have been, close friends. Such furnishings are of more than functional value; they have a deep personal significance. They too have their spatial demands.

So the scheme for the new house is a dichotomy: it is both a manifestation of the primal dwelling, and a spacious waterfront home of abundant amenities.

The scheme George has developed envisions that a one-car garage, on the southern half of the lot, will be seen from the sidewalk, and little else. The house itself will be, in essence, carved into the swale; the surface of its sod roof, north of and beyond the garage, will be well below eye level, about three feet above the plane of the sidewalk. To enter the house, one will move through a narrow and windowless passage that is part of the garage volume, to emerge at a glass-walled stair that descends to the floor plane of a dining space, about nine feet below the sidewalk elevation. The sea is not yet seen. A massive fireplace directly ahead is open on two sides, so a fire would be seen from the foot of the stair.

Eastward, directly under the garage and entry passage, will be the master (and only) bedroom and bath. A full-height window and a glazed pivoting panel are to open in the north wall to a view, across a shallow pool, to the side of the swale into which the house is carved. This bedroom will be a primordial cave, though a notably well-appointed one—a refuge within the earth, its outlook a view of extremely short reach.

North and west of the bedroom the swale will be abutted by another volume that is to contain the kitchen, a powder room, and a sleeping space for a guest. This volume and that of the bedroom lie at the edges of a rectangular glass-walled pavilion, the major space of the house, centered on the massive fireplace. The floor of the pavilion descends three steps as one moves seaward, past the fireplace, and as one moves farther seaward the architecture seems to simplify; glass opens the space to the site in all directions. Appropriately, the space is to end with Kim's piano; music, that most primordial, pervasive, and timeless of the arts, and the most sophisticated, too, resolves the dichotomy. The pavilion's floor plane continues beyond the glass. Steps descend to a third floor plane, entirely outside the pavilion's glass walls, and partly outside the edge of the pavilion's sod roof. This third floor plane bridges the swale not far above the level of the sea toward which it looks. On this simple terrace, at the edge of the land and the edge of the sea, open to sun and storm, more elemental than even the fisherman's cottage, the primal may be most nearly approached.

Epigraph: Oliver Sacks, *Musicophilia* (New York: Vintage, 2007, 2008), p. 217.

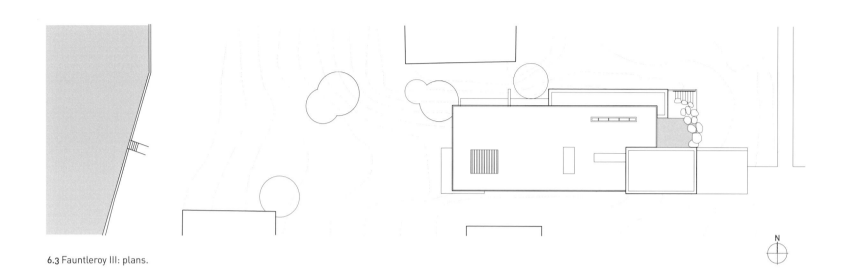

6.3 Fauntleroy III: plans.

N

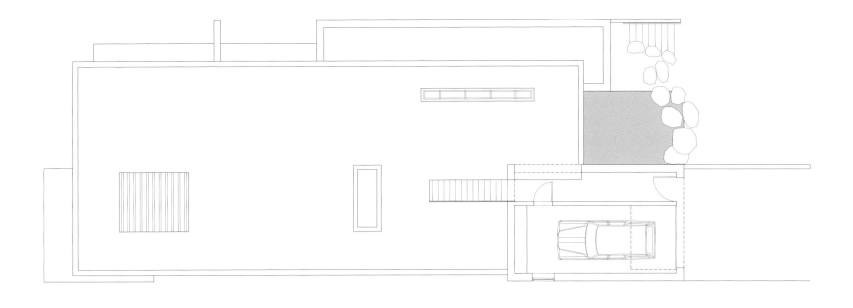

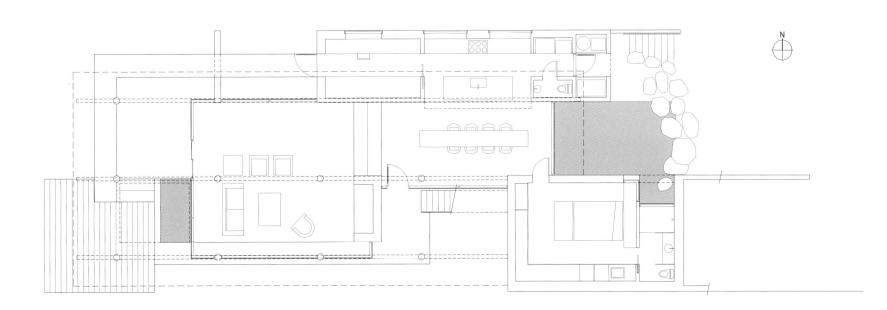

Fauntleroy III

# Epilogue

George Suyama is an unusually modest person. He is unlikely to write an autobiography; Kim says that he has wondered whether he deserves this book. He is always quick to acknowledge the contributions of others: Gene Zema, Ralph Anderson, Jean Jongeward, Jim Olson, Drake Salladay, Kurt Beardslee, David Gulassa, Bruce Hinckley; above all his partners Ric Peterson and Jay Deguchi. Equally, however, those others will insist that George is the conductor of the symphony.

Early in the development of this book, George was asked what buildings he most admired. He answered, only many months later, "Katsura. It is utterly rigorous and utterly free; it is nothing at all, and everything one wants or needs. Its beauty is a seemingly effortless beauty of the seemingly minimal. And it, and its setting, are one."

The Katsura villa might also be said to be a building whose exterior form is serendipitous, entirely a consequence of materials, structure, and interior dispositions, and this can also be said of Suyama's work. His interest in architecture began with the redecorating of his college-days room, a project, however rudimentary, in interior design. That aspect of the design task would not have been much encouraged in his college classes, but it may be meaningful that the class he most clearly remembers from those days was one of furniture design. In his employment with Gene Zema he was, perhaps for the first time, exposed to unique and dramatic interiors, those of Zema's Laurelhurst house above all; and in his employment with Ralph Anderson, he witnessed the importance of the role played by interior designer Jean Jongeward. This emphasis on the interior has deepened with time, but toward a particular objective: Suyama says that architecture's purpose is as "a tool that might allow one to live in a different and better way." That better way is to be realized through the freedom of a seeming simplicity of accommodation.

To an emphasis on the architectural interior Suyama has increasingly added a deep concern for the integration of interior spaces with the landscape; this, rather than a consideration of the building's exterior as a sculptural form, now determines the exterior character of his work. This predilection was augmented by Suyama's experiences in Japan—as suggested by his comments on Katsura, above—and, in later years, by his close association with landscape architects, foremost among them Bruce Hinckley. Thus it is impossible to envision the Schuchart or Fauntleroy houses as large-scale sculptural objects, nor is it easy to imagine for them any façade. They are more experiences than objects, and they are best understood not from any static viewpoint but by means of movement through their spaces, including their exterior spaces, if in fact interior and exterior can be meaningfully distinguished. The two structures of the McAdams retreat are rare instances of preordained exterior forms, and both forms are associated, in one way and another, with the landscape, the roof of the main house deriving from the boulders and dunes of the immediate site; the guest house "bunker," from the early-twentieth-century military coast emplacements of the region.

Suyama says that he seeks simplicity and serenity. Yet any perception of simplicity in his buildings is an illusion; his buildings are complicated things. We have noted the ambiguities and multivalences in his own house: the entry that is a garden gate; the room that is or is not a room; the cabinets that are many other things; the stair that belongs to the major volume under the simple rectangular roof—or is it part of the inserted bedroom box? How does such complexity yield serenity? Suyama says, "the complexities of twenty-first century building must be controlled and distilled to a visual peace and simplicity." Foremost among his means to control and distill, and thereby to yield a sense, if not the actuality, of simplicity, is his assiduous avoidance of other than straightforward geometries. He uses no doubly curved surfaces— the signature feature of Frank Gehry's designs. He uses none of Daniel Liebeskind's or Ove Arup's skewed geometries, nor the evident biological sources that inform Santiago Calatrava's thinking. Even cylindrical forms are rare in Suyama's work: they are found, in plan, only in the Benaroya condominium; in section, only in the McAdams retreat and the arches and ceiling vaults of the Grinstein house. The only non-90-degree geometries are in section, in Suyama's ubiquitous sloping roof planes, and there the motive is pragmatic, not formal. A simple order therefore always pervades all complexities, as a pervasive theme may cohere the vast complexities of a concerto, yielding, in each case, serenity. So it is that visitors to the Schuchart house most often describe its spaces as "tranquil," and Scott and Frances McAdams refer to their island retreat as "a place of perfect peace." Kim Suyama speaks of George's purpose as "serenity always, from our first apartment—serenity through interiors and the landscape."

Suyama's involvement with the arts has been long-standing: he has served, at various times, on the Pike Place Market Board, the Board of Directors for the University of Washington's Henry Art Gallery, the Goodwill Games Arts Commission, the Board of Directors for the theater group On the Boards; and he was for two terms a member of the Seattle Arts Commission. He founded "Suyama Space" shortly after he moved his architectural practice into the office on Second Avenue, and he announced its first installation in 1998.

In an architectural sense, Suyama Space is the central volume of Suyama's architectural office. The old and worn wooden floor remains from its days as the main workspace of the auto repair shop, as do the exposed roof trusses twenty feet overhead. The generous volume, with its workaday materials and surfaces, was almost ideally suited to its new purpose. It was modified for that purpose in just two ways. Since the space is windowless, Suyama opened large skylights along both the eastern and western edges, although the large volume, and the dark, relatively rough surfaces, yield a muted light on even the brightest days. The second modification is the inserted restrooms in the north end of the space, their walls made of a gridded, white, translucent plastic that admits a gentle modicum of light to the otherwise lightless rooms.

In an organizational sense, Suyama Space is a group of contributors who support artists' installations in the space. They include the Allen Foundation for the Arts, the Washington State Arts Commission, the King County Arts Commission, Space.City, and numerous individual contributors. Suyama is the titular director of Suyama Space, but he eagerly delegates the de facto direction to curator Beth Sellars.

The mission of Suyama Space is to provide "opportunities for experimentation, inspiration, and education in contemporary art . . . to serve as a catalyst in the creation of significant new works," collaborating with the art community to "expand public interest and understanding of contemporary art. We wanted to exhibit art that would challenge, inspire, and enlighten the public. We planned a place to show art that would otherwise have very little chance of exposure in Seattle. The space would be open to public view, yet would not be a sales gallery."* Thus Suyama Space emphasizes the work of artists who "demonstrate an innovative style and vision combined with an awareness of social,

**Cris Bruch**, *Duty Cycle*
June 9–August 18, 2000

cultural, and political issues." It also emphasizes installations that "respond to the gallery's unusual physical structure rather than introduce independently created works. The most successful installations have been those by artists who took clues from the architecture and allowed it to speak to them in their installation response."

The following is a representative selection of eight of the thirty-two installations that have been mounted to the time of this writing; they are organized chronologically. Quotations are drawn, and interpretations paraphrased, from the brochures that were prepared to accompany each work.

Created for Suyama Space, Bruch's installation seemed a manifestation of its surroundings. *Duty Cycle* was a disk, 17 feet in diameter and 32 inches thick, made of long, diamond-shaped pieces of un-waxed, milk-carton paper glued together around a bearing assembly at the hub. Suspended by a single cable, the resultant wheel turned at a touch. A single 14-inch hole near the perimeter offered a glimpse of the internal engineering; a collection of old metal buckets surrounding the wheel caught water dripping from tubes concealed in the roof structure. In its context of the rough floor planks and the equally rough concrete walls of the ancient car-repair shop, Bruch's wheel seemed a ghostly apparition from one of Leonardo's notebooks.

**Yuriko Yamaguchi,** *Metamorphosis/Web*
1 February–5 April 2002

Yamaguchi's creation consisted of two bodies of work, of which *Web* is shown here. *Web* comprised several hundred hand-formed pods of flax, abaca, and wire hung from the gallery ceiling by invisible filament lines. The pods, clustered at eye level, paradoxically suggested both a place of ritual and a swarm of natural forms.

**John Bisbee**, *Three Tons*
3 May–16 August 2002

The title simply refers to the cumulative weight of three complementary compositions; a criterion for each of the three was that it be constructed of 2,000 pounds of steel. One of the compositions, *Plume*, was an array of "tufts" of spikes spread across the translucent-panel wall and encroaching on the adjacent floor, "as delicate as the growth of vegetable life . . . each spike like a blade of grass under a strong wind." *Plode* was a group of ten spheres, each formed of hundreds of spikes radiating from a central core. *Arc* would seem to have mediated the other two compositions, as an assemblage of spikes whose arcs turned and twisted into configurations evoking both vines and spheres.

**Kazuo Kadonaga**, *Pure Form*
6 January–11 April 2003

**Katy Stone**, *Degrees of Appearance*
October 6 2003–January 9 2004

On entry, one faced, across the opening in the far wall, a screen of shiny bamboo shafts holding court, as it were, for various forms of wood, bamboo, and paper, in part left in their intrinsic natural forms, and in part evidencing human modification. "These pieces, born in Japan, have traveled widely in the United States and Europe for a number of years; distances and changes in geography matter only to the extent that climate comes to bear on the work—because changes in heat and humidity greatly affect the materials . . . accumulation of time compounds climatic variations and can change the appearance as well as the structure . . . divulging salient properties."

Katy Stone's installation derived, in part, from Katsushika Hokusai's woodblock prints, "pictures of the floating world." Stone, like Hokusai, sought not simply an illustration or rendering of a landscape, but rather a restatement of the energy residing in the forces of nature—ideas of rushing water, swooshing swarms, spreading roots, wispy willows, bulbous droplets, fluid blades, preserved in perpetuity.

**Trimpin**, *SHHH*
1 May–28 July 2006

"According to legend, initiates seeking to become followers of Pythagoras had to listen to the master's teaching from behind a curtain. Such sensory reduction supposedly focused the attention, leaving hearing as the sole conduit for new ideas." In homage to Pythagoras, *SHHH*, a metal ball of brushed aluminum (its finish a cliché of contemporary décor) rolls within a circular caged track painted an industrial gray-blue, translating into circular motion musical ratios traditionally demonstrated on a single, stretched string atop a movable bridge.

**John Grade**, *Seeps of Winter*
January 21–April 18, 2008

*Seeps of Winter* is a graceful, if enormous, gray mass suspended from the 20-foot ceiling of Suyama Space. Spreading corner to corner over the room's 1,500 square feet, its surface is covered with gray paper pulp. It appears to billow in the center of the space, dipping ominously as low as the height of a short adult. Hundreds of small openings at odd intervals diffuse any illumination cast from the skylight above so that walking underneath the pieces is disorienting. . . .While *Seeps of Winter* was inspired in part by the bogs of western Ireland, its scale and formal beauty are stripped of any association but their own formidable presence. Grade's installation was the epitome of the mission statement for Suyama Space, i.e., the artist is required to respond directly to the physical architecture of the space; as Grade explains, *Seeps of Winter* is "an interior architectural space that is inspired by one natural landscape, and then placed in another actual (but different) landscape."

**Dan Corson**, *Grotesque Arabesque*
September 21–December 18, 2009

*Grotesque Arabesque* is the culminating expression of Dan Corson's cave explorations in the Yucatan. He describes the stalactites dipping low to the floors of the giant vaulted caverns, while filtered shafts of light streamed through cracks in the rock high above, to create a vibrating azure blue glow, its reflection distorted in the pooled water, confusing the defining edges of the cave.

Corson abstracted the cave's contours as a series of vertical sections. The computer morphed these into one another, creating a topographical progression that is simulated in the installation by steel strips suspended across the gallery's ceiling, each individually illuminated by green-glowing electroluminescent tape. The large pond below this soaring green topography both replicates and distorts that topography through shifting, rippling reflections.

Although we have a long-standing tendency to associate art with beauty, art is seldom addressed to beauty alone, may not be at all concerned with beauty, whatever that may be, and "beautiful," itself an elastic and ill-defined term, is seldom used in art criticism. Yet there are occasions in which an artistic creation cries out for those words. In *Grotesque Arabesque*, Dan Corson has created an experience of remarkable beauty, a strikingly beautiful thing.

*George Suyama, "Preface," in *Wind: A Sound Translation by Patrick Zentz*, the brochure for the installation of May 7–July 22, 1999.

# Appendix II

## PRODUCT DESIGN: THE 3 × 10 SHOP

Suyama's earliest design interest was in furnishings, and the 3 × 10 shop is a late manifestation of that interest. He established the shop in 2002, in the northern half of the office's street-front spaces, to offer a retail source for a wide variety of design products, most of them, in one way or another, home furnishings. Some are "one-of-a-kind finds" gathered during extensive travel throughout Europe and Asia; others are fabricated to Suyama Peterson Deguchi's designs. Originally George had hoped that some of the office's staff might work on such designs, but the press of work has foreclosed that possibility. The pieces illustrated are continuously available, but as the following images suggest, the shop's inventory is serendipitous. The guiding philosophy is contrary to that of normal merchandising within our culture, in that everything in the shop is a product of a craft; nothing is mass-produced. In this, the shop is one with the firm's philosophy of architecture, but many of the shop's artifacts, free of obligations to structure, site, and program, can represent a more pure expression of that philosophy.

**Above:** Drum lamp, bent steel tables, fireplace tools, grate, and square steel vase.
George Suyama designs, 3 x 10 Collection

**Opposite:** 3 x 10 showroom: the door at center opens to Suyama Space

Stanchion floor lamp. George Suyama design, 3 x 10 Collection

Round steel tray. George Suyama design, 3 x 10 Collection

Nutcracker and bent steel table. George Suyama designs, 3 x 10 Collection

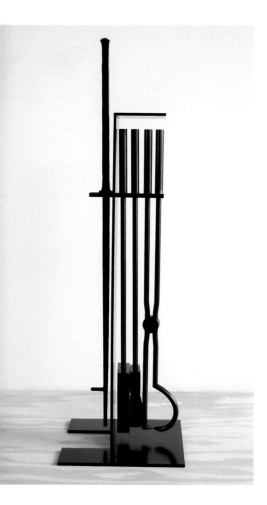

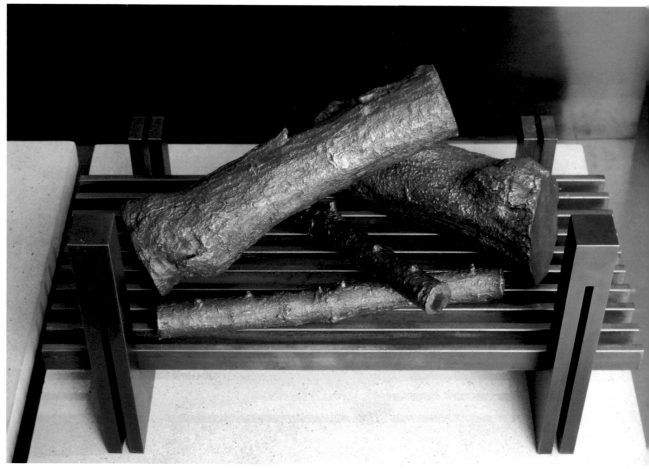

Fireplace tools. George Suyama design, 3 x 10 Collection

Fireplace grate with bronze logs. George Suyama design, 3 x 10 Collection

3 x 10, with book press, bent steel
tables, floor candlesticks, live edge plank,
and Scott Fife's archival cardboard sculpture
of Marion Robert Morrison (aka John
Wayne), 2007

# Appendix III

## SIGNIFICANT PROJECTS AND AWARDS THROUGH 2009

Architectural projects, from inception to occupancy, or even from inception to letting of contracts, seldom fit neatly within a calendar year. Dates given below are dates of inception.

**1972–89**
Starbucks Coffee shops (8), Seattle, WA

**1973**
Suyama house, Madison Park (remodel), Seattle, WA

**1979**
Garside house (remodel), Seattle, WA
Salladay Pike Place Flowers (second shop), Seattle, WA
Suyama house, Broadway (remodel), Seattle, WA

**1979–99**
Peet's Coffee & Tea shops (14), California

**1982**
George Suyama Architects, East Boston office, Seattle, WA

**1983**
Benaroya condominium, Seattle, WA

**1985**
FORMA headquarters, Seattle, WA
Nelly Stallion shop, University District, Seattle, WA
LEL Ltd. office, Seattle, WA

**1986**
Lumpkin house, Seattle, WA
Nordstrom condominium, Seattle, WA
Suyama house ("Fauntleroy I"), Seattle, WA

**1987**
Milgard house, Allen Point, WA

**1988**
Daniel Louis Jewelry shop, Seattle, WA
Hurlbut house, Mercer Island, WA

**1989**
Berde house, Seattle, WA
Campbell house, Vancouver, WA
Hall houseboat, Seattle, WA

**1990**
Martin house (unbuilt), Des Moines, WA

**1991**
Belltown Billiards, Seattle, WA
Dorsey house, Seattle, WA
Japanese Congregational Church, Seattle, WA
Jefferts/Squires house, Shaw Island, WA
Schultz house, Seattle, WA
Traver Gallery, Seattle, WA

**1992**
Kemper cabin, Mount Vernon, WA
Mayberg house, Seattle, WA

**1993**
Ershig house, Bellingham, WA
Hornall house, Vashon Island, WA
Jefferts retreat, Shaw Island, WA
Michael house, Woodway, WA
Rosen house, Seattle, WA

**1994-97**
Fonté Coffee Roaster shops (5), Juneau, Chicago, Los Angeles

**1995**
Eisenberg/Kadowaki house, Seattle, WA
Leland house, Seattle, WA

**1996**
Borracchini house, Seattle, WA
Everett house, Sun Valley, ID
Guy house, Seattle, WA
Lockwood retreat, Lopez Island, WA
On the Boards Theatre, Seattle, WA

**1997**
Grevstad/Draheim retreat, Decatur Island, WA
George Suyama Architects, Second Avenue Office, Seattle, WA
The Orchard, Medina, WA

**1998**
Grinstein house, Medina, WA
McAdams retreat, San Juan Island, WA
Suyama house ("Fauntleroy II"), Seattle, WA

**1999**
Baldwin house, Sonoma, CA

**2000**
Frontier Room, Seattle, WA
Jefferts/Hutchins house, Shaw Island, WA

**2001**
3 × 10 showroom, Seattle, WA
Bridge house, Seattle, WA

**2002**
McQuarrie house, Seattle, WA

**2003**
Nisei Veterans' Hall, Seattle, WA
Plymouth Café, Seattle, WA
Piggott house, Seattle, WA
Schuchart house, Seattle, WA
Solazzi houseboat, Seattle, WA

**2004**
4Culture offices and gallery, Seattle, WA
Kemp house, Neskowin, OR
Kotkins house, Seattle, WA
True/Brown house, Seattle, WA

**2005**
Benaroya house, Newport Shores, WA
Kaplan house, Mercer Island, WA
Michael house, Bainbridge Island, WA
Utterberg condominium, Seattle, WA
Gengé/Perry kit house, Salt Spring Island, BC

**2007**
McDougall house, Medina, WA
Condominium for an anonymous client, Bellevue, WA

**2008**
House for an anonymous client (interior design only),
with Kengo Kuma, Tokyo, Japan

**2009**
Grinstein retreat, Indianola, WA
Suyama house (Fauntleroy III) (unbuilt project), Seattle, WA

## Honors

1993    Elected to College of Fellows, American Institute of Architects
2004    University of Washington Libraries Artist of the Year
2009    AIA Seattle Medal of Honor for distinguished lifetime achievement
2009    Seattle Homes and Lifestyles Design Achievement Award in Architecture

## Selected Awards

1990    AIA Seattle Citation, "Future" category, Martin house
1996    Wood Council National Design Award, Kemper cabin
1997    AIA Seattle Honor Award, George Suyama Architects Second Avenue
         office and Suyama Space gallery
2003    AIA Seattle Honor Award, Suyama house (Fauntleroy II)
2004    AIA Northwest Honor Award, Suyama house (Fauntleroy II)
2005    AIA Seattle Honor Award, Schuchart house
2006    AIA Northwest Honor Award, Schuchart house
2009    International Interior Design Association Honorable Mention,
         Schuchart house
2009    International Interior Design Association Concept Design Award,
         Stanchion floor lamp
2009    International Interior Design Association Concept Design Award,
         Fireplace tool set

# Contributing Personnel

Bob Asahara
Randy Bemis
Patricia Bittner
Andrew Borges
Paula Calderon
William Caramella
Stephen Chiatovich
Sergio Chin-Ley
Ralph Christiansen
Gilles Cullie
James Cutler
Jay Deguchi
David Derrer
Laura Doll
Daren Doss
Tyler Engle
Heidi Epstein
David Evans
Zana Faulkner
John Fleming
David Gilchrist
Jim Goodspeed
Bill Haas
Chris Haddad
Knut Hanson
Ranette Hart
Wes Hoffman
Allison Hogue
Sean Kakigi
Steve Kern
Jeff King
Chris Kim
Mark Kolmodin
Louise Lakier
Kim Lavacot

Steven Lazen
Jeff Luth
Sarah MacDonald
Carl Mahaney
Rune Martinson
Robin Meyer
Colleen Miller
Kevin Miyamura
Cassandra Montgomery
Miye Moriguchi
Kazu Murata
Susan Olmsted
Matthias Olt
Jim Nakata
Ric Peterson
Kim Pham
John Phillips
Scott Rae
Erik Remash
Alex Rhode
Dennis Rooks
Aya Sakurai
Matt Scholl
Cindy Selkirk
Nancy Shoji
Emma Shultz
Jym Snedeker
Kevin Sokoloski
Peter Spruance
Aubrey Summers
Kim Suyama
John Trieger
Michio Valian
Andres Villaveces
Bill Voss

Jenny Waddell
Jeff Wilson
Laurel Wilson
Debi Yeabsley
Dahlia Zuniga

# Major Donors

# Image Credits

1.1–1.8, 1.13–1.16: Grant Hildebrand

1.9, 3.1, 6.1, 6.2: Suyama Peterson Deguchi; Steven Lazen

1.10: Don Normark

1.11, 1.12: Dick Busher

2.1–2.3, 2.16: Chris Eden

2.4, 2.5: John Vaughan

2.6–2.9, 2.15, 2.18, 2.27, 2.33, 2.38–2.41, 3.6, 3.16, 3.29, 4.1, 4.3, 4.4: George Suyama Architects

2.10, 2.12: Michael Jensen

2.11: Haruo Komiya

2.13, 2.25, 2.26, 2.28–2.31: David Story

2.14, 2.17, 2.19–2.22: Michael Shopenn

2.23, 2.24: Norman McGrath

2.32, 2.34–2.37, 3.26–3.28, 3.30–3.32, 3.35, 3.37, 3.38, 3.44, 3.45, 3.46, 3.50, 3.53, 4.4, 4.5–4.9, 4.13, 4.14, 5.8–5.11, 5.21: Paul Warchol

3.2–3.4, 5.1, 5.15, 5.16: Claudio Santini

front cover, 3.5, 3.7–3.12, 3.13–3.15, 3.17–3.25, 3.40, 3.41, 3.43, 3.49, 3.51, 3.54, 3.56, 3.57, 4.9, 4.10, 4.11, 4.12, 4.15: Michael Burns

3.39, 5.4, 5.5, 6.3, p. 163: Suyama Peterson Deguchi

3.42, 3.46, 3.47, 3.48, 3.52, 3.55: Suyama Peterson Deguchi; Chris Haddad

4.2: Sound View Aerial Photography

3.33, 3.34, 3.36, 5.2, 5.3: Suyama Peterson Deguchi; George Suyama

5.6, 5.7, 5.12–5.14, 5.18, 9.7: Lara Swimmer

5.17, 5.19, 5.20: Grey Crawford

p. 3: Paul Warchol (same photo as 5.10)

p. 142: Richard Nicol

p. 143: Cris Bruch

pp. 144–148: Eduardo Calderón

p. 149: John Grade

pp. 150–51: Dan Corson

pp. 154–159: Suyama Peterson Deguchi; Sarah MacDonald

Special thanks to the photographers who kindly provided extra service to make this publication possible.

Chris Bruch

Michael Burns

Dick Busher

Eduardo Calderón

Dan Corson

Grey Crawford

John Grade

Michael Jensen

Norman McGrath

Richard Nicol

Don Normark

Michael Shopenn

David Story

Lara Swimmer

Paul Warchol

# Index